IMAGES

of America

THE COPACABANA

Joe E. Lewis, then the most beloved and biggest name in nightclub entertainment, is shown keeping a wartime audience in good spirits in a New Years Eve 1942 photograph by George Karger. The famous legs and beguiling smiles of the Copa Girls augment the exotic, South American–flavored scenery, capturing the essence of the Copacabana nightclub in its heyday. (Courtesy of Time Life Pictures/Getty Images.)

ON THE COVER: The boy and girl production singers, dancer Dee Turnell (center), and the beautiful Copa Girls in their exquisite costumes perform to the sounds of the Copacabana orchestra as a rapt, well-dressed audience looks on, conveying the overall thrill and excitement of a Copa floor show in a July 1, 1944, photograph by Eileen Darby. (Courtesy of Time Life Pictures/Getty Images.)

IMAGES
of America

THE COPACABANA

Kristin Baggelaar

ARCADIA
PUBLISHING

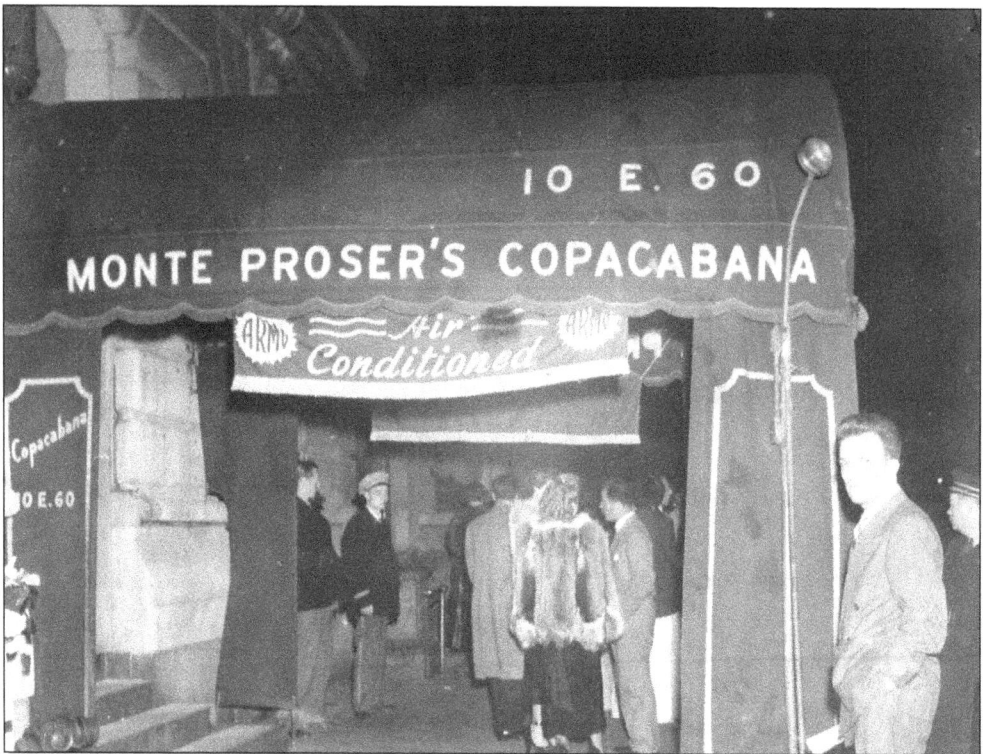

One of the first concerns to install air conditioning in movie houses and in Macy's department store in the late 1930s was Armo Air Conditioning and Cooling Company. Its banner proudly advertises the climate-controlled comfort at the Copacabana in an undated photograph. In the early years, prior to air conditioning, the Copa closed during the hot summer months. (Courtesy of Frank Driggs.)

CONTENTS

ACKNOWLEDGMENTS

A book about a nightclub is essentially a book about people, and there are many individuals to whom I wish to express my appreciation for their time, knowledge, and for sharing with me their memories of and feelings for the Copacabana. I am particularly grateful for assistance, information, and/or images provided by Toni Arden, Maxine Barrat Carter, Reni Churchill, Errol Dante, Frank Driggs, Holly Foster-Wells at Peggy Lee Enterprises, Ed Gottlieb, Lauren Gurgiolo at the Harry Ransom Humanities Research Center, the University of Texas at Austin, Ed Hertel, Don Hunstein, John Juliano, Albert Kopec, Frankie Laine, Mike Moran, Dan Morgenstern, Edna Ryan Murcott, Pat Niglio, Brendan O'Brien, Evelyn Peterson Ohlrich, Nancy Rattenbury at Queens Museum, Fran Morris Rosman at the Ella Fitzgerald Charitable Foundation, Jimmy Scalia, Al Stewart, Sonni Strenke, Alice Syman, Morty Trautman, Judy Varley of the Society of Singers, and Kathy War at the University of Nevada, Las Vegas.

For so graciously giving me access to her personal scrapbooks, I am greatly indebted to Society of Singers's East Coast Chapter president and former Copa production singer Terri Stevens Norbeck, whose backstage snapshots provide a first-hand look at what it was like behind the scenes of a world-famous nightclub.

I also wish to acknowledge the resources and cooperation of the staff of the New York Public Library, in particular the Performing Arts' Billy Rose Theatre Collection, Jerome Robbins Dance Division, and the Art and Architecture/Miriam and Ira D. Wallach Division of Art, Prints and Photographs. Also unsurpassed in generosity and spirit was AP Images sales representative Jorge A. Jaramillo, who traversed the Copacabana archives to tease out the pictures that tell its story.

And, of course, I am grateful to my editor, Erin Vosgien, who kept me on course.

INTRODUCTION

In its time, the 1940s and 1950s, the long-ago glamorous Copacabana was the biggest, best-known, and most popular nightclub in Manhattan. Some contend it was the most popular nightclub *ever*. In the pseudo-tropical atmosphere, you would ogle the Copa Girls, strain your eyes to see who was sitting at the best tables, and then read about it the next day in Walter Winchell's column.

No other club had a greater impact on talent and café operations across the nation than the Copacabana. No other club did as much to develop acts as well as managerial talent. The Copa was the bellwether of the nitery business throughout the country and the pinnacle of showbiz ambition for every café act in the business.

The Copa is a storehouse of memories that evokes a nostalgic, yet unsentimental, backward glance at the years that have come and gone. These were the thrilling years of an incredible entertainment era. It was the heyday of nightlife in New York and the Copacabana epitomized the madcap fun and excitement of those high-living days. It was a celebrity hangout—a place to be seen, as well as to see that celebrated audience, the stars of the stage and screen—Elizabeth Taylor, Mike Todd, Louis B. Mayer, Marlene Dietrich, Errol Flynn, and Bette Davis. They were all there regularly, like the pulsating, electric, opening night in 1954 when a standing-room-only celebrity-packed audience flipped over an established star, Frank Sinatra, and cheered and made a new star of Joey Bishop. In the audience were all the names that made headline news; Judy Garland, Yul Brenner, Edith Piaf, Dinah Shore, Sammy Davis Jr., Jane Kean, Johnnie Ray, Nanette Fabray, and Sugar Ray Robinson.

The Copa's roster of performers read like a who's who of show business. Copa boss Jules Podell followed in the footsteps of originator Monte Proser with an uncanny knack for picking unknown talent that went on to stardom, such as Perry Como, Johnny Mathis, Bobby Darin, and Paul Anka. Sammy Davis Jr. achieved his dream in the spring of 1954 when the Will Mastin Trio featured him while they made their New York café debut at the Copacabana. The team of Dean Martin and Jerry Lewis, along with Tony Bennett, Julie Wilson, Wayne Newton, and many others who are still big names today, got their first big break at the Copa and made their emotional, final appearance together there.

No other nightclub had a more profound effect on the public recognition of a performer than the Copacabana. A comedian didn't *arrive* until he scored at the Copa. Singers assured their future prestige by continually doing well there.

The Copacabana was also the springboard to star status and the silver screen for the beautiful Copa Girls. From June Allyson, who taught herself to dance as a girl by watching the footwork in MGM musicals, and went from the Copa Girl line to Hollywood stardom and into the arms of actor Dick Powell; to acclaimed actress-dancer Lucille Bremer; Jane Ball, who won the heart of and married Copa founder-owner Monte Proser; actress Grace Gillern; Janice Rule, on screen from 1951 and married for 25 years to actor Ben Gazzara; Barbara Feldon, who became famous for her role in the television series *Get Smart*; singer-actress Julie Wilson, who became a veritable cabaret cottage industry, and so on.

Whether or not you've lived through this era, it is possible to feel a yearning for it, an urge to call back a way of life now gone forever—the golden years of fabulous, unforgettable nights, nights of laughter, nights of excitement. The Copa takes us back, even if we were never there.

Many years have passed since the opening of the Copacabana and while those years have seen much change, this landmark institution continues to symbolize everything that is understood to be cosmopolitan, elegant, and glamorous. The world-famous Copacabana, a mainstay of New York clubs' golden era, lives on in the public's imagination.

One

A Prelude to a Piece of Musical History
1940

The Copacabana burst on the scene over half a century ago as the Great Depression was ending and World War II was beginning. While the United States was no longer in the Depression, many citizens had not yet recovered from it. The country was moving closer to war, but temporarily still at peace. It was a tense, highly dramatic period of history. Americans were wrestling with insecurity and indecision as they nervously awaited changes that might affect their work, homes, and family lives. The menacing possibility of direct involvement in the war evoked fear and sorrow as well as excitement, and doubts about the future stimulated a craving for pleasure. While America was not immediately endangered or officially embroiled in battle, prewar jitters pervaded, and a mood of unrestraint produced an upsurge in patronage of hotels, restaurants, movie houses, theaters, and nightclubs. The highly charged atmosphere recalled the frenetic pace of the Roaring Twenties, and again, the times were hot. (Courtesy of New York City Guide, 1939.)

Migration from rural to metropolitan areas continued as it had been for years, but now the pace was accelerating. Not since the upheaval of the French Revolution would so many talented, well-to-do, cultured refugees be brought together in this friendly haven at one time. They, in turn, would elevate the status of New York, establishing this great city beyond all doubt as the premier cultural capital of the United States. (Courtesy of New York City Guide, 1939.)

29W   *Fountain Lake Amphitheatre with Billy Rose's Aquacade on Stage, New York World's Fair*

The 1939 New York World's Fair, more than anything else, attracted the attention, not only of this country, but of the world, to New York City. Dance director of the popular Aquacade attraction, Robert (Bob) Alton, already known for his work with many theatrical and nightclub productions, would soon be hired as one of the Copacabana's original choreographers. (Courtesy of Billy Rose's Aquacade program.)

Future Copa headliner Carmen Miranda was fueling the Latin fever in New York with her explosive performance in the musical revue *Streets of Paris* (with dances and ensemble staged by Bob Alton). Once-popular, lavish Ziegfeld-type productions had fallen out of favor and it only followed that the increasingly popular format of a musical revue would carry over from the Broadway stage to the nightclub floor. Carmen Miranda is shown with Gloria Jean (left) in a 1947 *Copacabana* still photograph. (Courtesy of Gloria Jean.)

New York City, of course, played host to much more than Broadway. It was the heyday of big bands and boom years for ballrooms, where hundreds of patrons indulged in a cheek-to-cheek fox-trot, fast-danced a lindy, or jitterbugged to the hot sounds of swing. An undated promotional advertisement for Guy Lombardo, who played the "Sweetest Music this Side of Heaven" at the Roosevelt Grill, is shown here.

11

KEY TO TIMES SQUARE THEATER DISTRICT MAP

(The following are theaters, except Nos. 20, 33, and 89.)

1. Labor Stage
2. Maxine Elliott
3. Empire
4. Metropolitan Opera House
5. National
6. Mercury
7. Cameo
8. New Amsterdam
9. Sam H. Harris
10. Liberty
11. Eltinge
12. Wallach
13. Selwyn
14. Apollo
15. Times Square
16. Lyric
17. Republic
18. Rialto
19. Henry Miller
20. Town Hall
21. Hippodrome
22. Belasco
23. Hudson
24. Loew's Criterion
25. Paramount
26. Forty-fourth Street
27. Nora Bayes
28. Little
29. St. James
30. Majestic
31. Broadhurst
32. Shubert
33. Shubert Alley
34. Booth
35. Plymouth
36. CBS Radio Theater No. 1
37. John Golden
38. Martin Beck
39. CBS Radio Theater No. 2
40. Imperial
41. Music Box
42. Morosco
43. Bijou
44. Astor
45. Loew's State
46. Lyceum
47. Gaiety
48. Fulton
49. Forty-sixth Street
50. Mansfield
51. Central
52. Globe
53. Embassy
54. Palace
55. Cort
56. Vanderbilt
57. Loew's Mayfair
58. Strand
59. Ethel Barrymore
60. Biltmore
61. Longacre
62. Forty-eighth Street
63. Ritz
64. Rivoli
65. Windsor
66. Playhouse
67. Belmont
68. Center
69. World
70. Translux
71. Forrest
72. Cinema 49
73. CBS Radio Theater No. 4
74. Capitol
75. Winter Garden
76. Roxy
77. Music Hall
78. Continental
79. Hollywood
80. Alvin
81. Guild
82. Cine Roma
83. Loew's Ziegfeld
84. Adelphi
85. CBS Radio Theater No. 3
86. New Yorker
87. Fifty-fifth Street Playhouse
88. Little Carnegie Playhouse
89. Carnegie Hall
90. Filmarte
91. Yiddish Art

W. 60th ST.   COI
W. 59th ST.
W. 58th
W. 57th
W. 56th
W. 55th
W. 54th
W. 53rd
W. 52nd
W. 51st
W. 50th
W. 49th
W. 48th
W. 47th
W. 46th
W. 45th
38
W. 44th
W. 43rd
W. 42nd
W. 41st
W. 40th

TIM

THEA

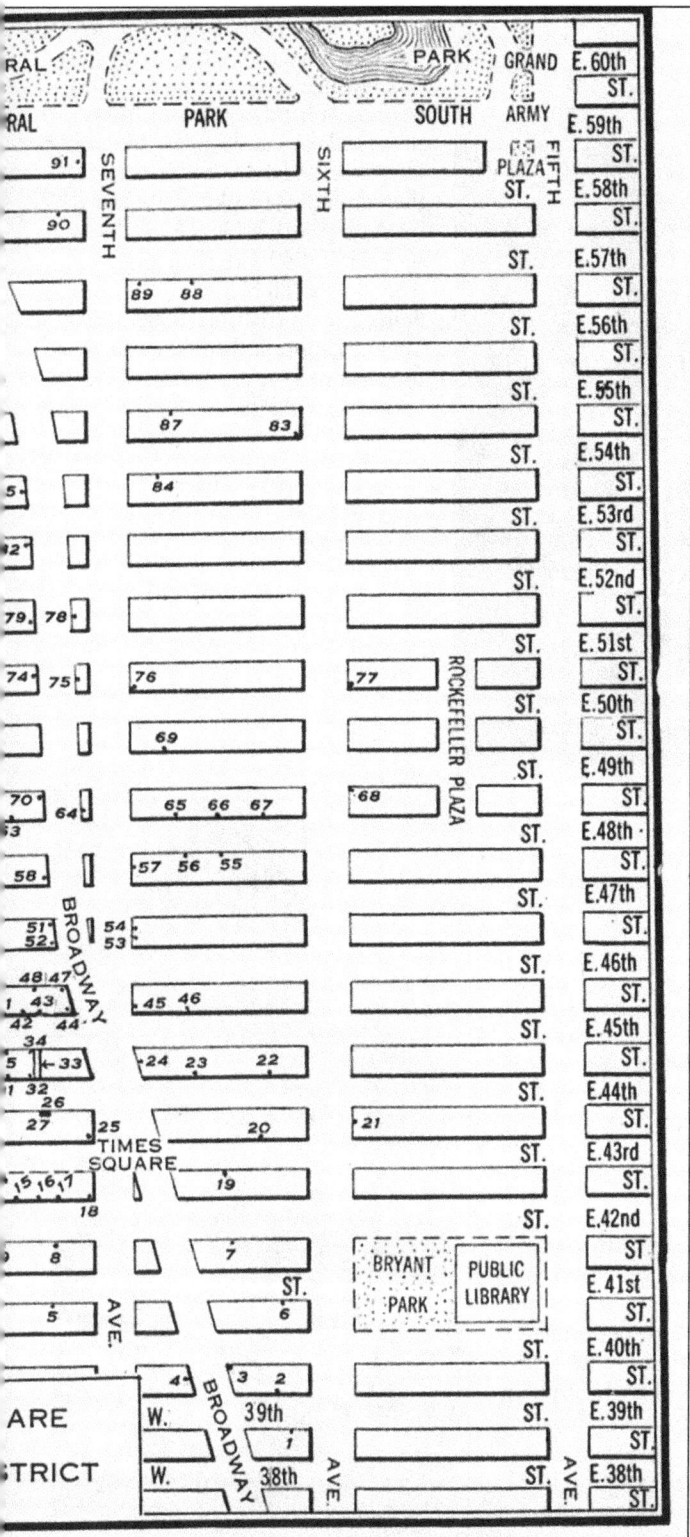

New York City had entertainment for every taste. Its nightlife ranged from variety and vaudeville stage shows to legitimate theater, ballet, and opera. Tourists from all walks of life were lured by the vast array of big-city offerings. Moving within the entertainment circuit in New York, it was hard to believe that a war was escalating in Europe or that America was still feeling the ravages of the Depression. For so many years Times Square enjoyed a reputation as the hub of great hotels, restaurants, nightclubs, and theater. The nighttime sky blazed with the neon signs of Broadway, flickering like jewels, in the most brilliant display of lights in the world. Broadway, the symbol and showplace of American theater, was the heart, the soul, and the character of New York City—and the Copacabana would be only a short walk from Broadway to the East Side. (Courtesy of New York City Guide, 1939.)

In this heyday of big bands, only a handful of vocalists recorded on their own as singers were hired primarily to be another band instrument. When singer Jack Leonard left the Tommy Dorsey Band, he was replaced by a then-unknown Frank Sinatra, who hit the top of the charts in the early summer of 1940 with the Dorsey recording of "I'll Never Smile Again." Frank Sinatra (right) is shown with Tommy Dorsey at the RCA Victor Studios in a 1941 photograph. (Courtesy of AP Images.)

SEVENTH AVENUE at 50th STREET, NEW YORK

Although New York City was indisputably the entertainment capital of America, the $3.30-or-more ticket to a stage show or the even more expensive concert by a big-name performer was beyond the means of many citizens. One of the most popular and affordable forms of entertainment was the motion picture, at 25¢, which was shown at popular theaters like the Roxy. A prosperous Hollywood continued to reign as all-powerful in the entertainment industry in the United States. (Courtesy of Harry H. Baumann.)

While most Americans spent prime-time evening hours gathered around the family radio, a select few comprising of the ultra-chic, publicity-mad café society were creating the glamorous image of New York nightlife and packing its finest establishments. Nightclubs like the Colony, 21, and El Morocco became the hot spots of the day, along with the Stork Club, where gossip king Walter Winchell held court nightly at legendary Table 50 in the Cub Room, shown here. (Courtesy of AP Images.)

THE ONLY AUTHENTIC CUBAN-SPANISH RESTAURANT IN AMERICA

Other clubs combined the appeal of a nightclub with entertainment, such as the Hurricane, Diamond Horseshoe, Casa Manana, La Conga, La Martinique ("the upholstered sewer"). Shown here, Havana-Madrid was the rumba spot where, in 1949, 21-year-old Jerry Lewis was the opening act for 29-year-old crooner Dean Martin. (Courtesy of Colourpicture Publication.)

The many clubs on 52nd Street, between Fifth and Sixth Avenues, were also very popular. This famous jazz strip, known as Swing Street, was home to the Onyx, 88, Club 18, and Leon and Eddie's, where future Copa-ringsider, a young Jackie Gleason, was heralded in early 1941 as "New York's New Comedy Ace." (Courtesy of Harry H. Baumann.)

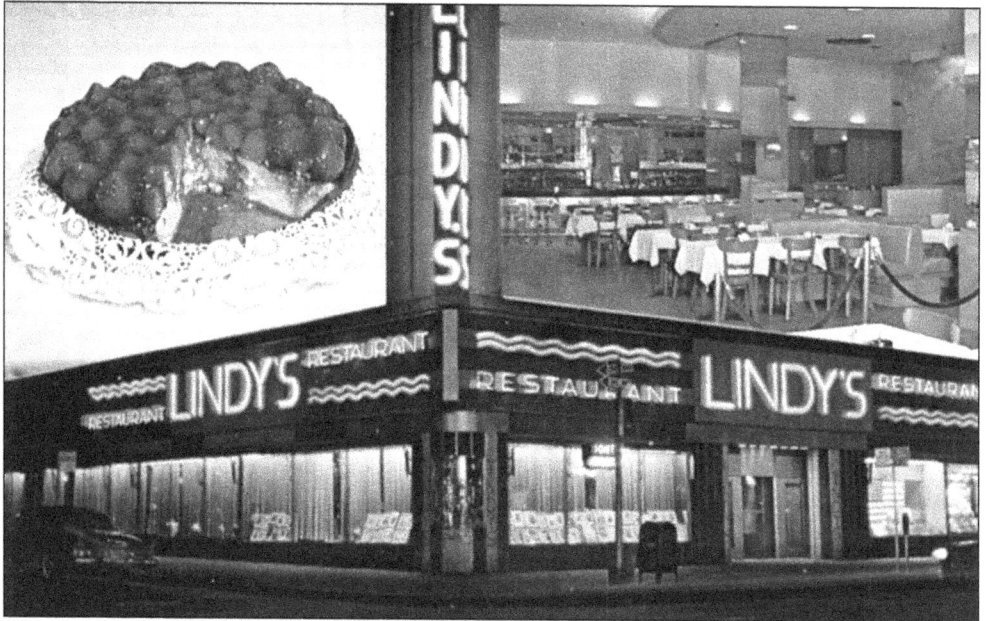

To bring in the crowds, nightclubs and restaurants hired press agents, who promoted their clients and provided "items" about stars of the screen and stage as well as society gadabouts to the all-powerful newspaper columnists of the day. The columnists, in turn, shaped the lives of those in want of the limelight. After-hours hangouts included the Stagedoor Deli, Reubens, and a Broadway landmark called Lindy's, which acquired a national reputation through the Broadway columnists for the gossip and celebrities that passed continually through its doors. (Courtesy of Bertil Carlson.)

16

The reputed "King of the Publicity World" in those days was a soft-spoken, unpretentious man named Monte Proser. He was hired as the Stork Club's first publicist and went on to publicize dozens of other nightspots in New York City. (Courtesy of AP Images.)

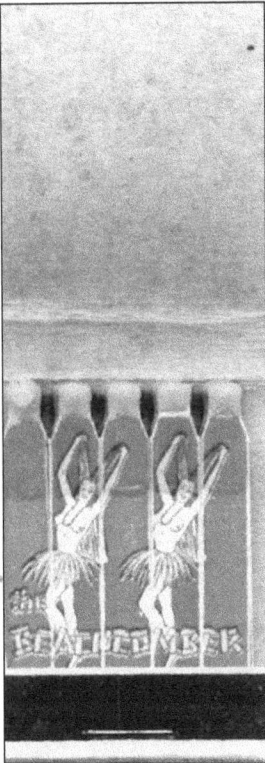

Monte Proser had his first success as a nightclub owner with La Conga in Hollywood. He returned to New York, where he set off a cycle of South Sea Island nightspots with the success of his first, Beachcomber—a Broadway high spot with a tropical décor and pretty, sarong-clad girls—followed by others in Providence, Miami Beach, and Boston. (Courtesy of Lion Match.)

The Copacabana was Monte Proser's first venture on Manhattan's Upper East Side. This section of old-money New York was also home to the exclusive Harmonie Club, the Colony Club for ladies and the Union Club for gentlemen, the Metropolitan Club, and a trio of the city's finest old hotels, the Sherry Netherland, the Pierre, and the Savoy-Plaza, shown here. (Courtesy of New York City Guide, 1939.)

The basement of the 13-story building occupied by the Hotel Fourteen, located at 14 East 60th Street, was chosen as the site for the Copacabana, shown in a 1940 tax photograph. The deal was announced in the real estate section of the *New York Times*, September 17, 1940. (Courtesy of NYC Municipal Archives.)

The location for the proposed Latin-American supper club was formerly C. Morton Bellak's nightclub, located at 10 East 60th Street. It later became the Villa Vallee restaurant, a dark, gloomy Prohibition club with mirrored walls that reflected the image, of its featured attraction, owner-crooner Rudy Vallee. The space involved in the lease to Monte Proser, president of Copacabana, Inc., was about 12,500 square feet and the total rental was said to be about $100,000. (Photograph by A. Eriss; courtesy of Country Press Inc.)

In his 1933 inaugural address, Pres. Franklin D. Roosevelt had declared a good neighbor policy, which spurred America's interest in Latin America. A Latin trend, started in the 1920s with the popularity of Rudolph Valentino, shown here, was in full swing. Its dances, the conga, rumba, and samba, were blossoming into a rage that would characterize the 1940s.

Latin music conjured up the romance and infectious joie de vivre of festive Rio de Janeiro. In those days, nightlife in the elegant Copacabana district of Brazil's capital was divided between the Cassino Atlantico, and the Copacabana at the Copacabana Palace Hotel. Monte Proser chose the latter as the model and name for his Upper East Side New York venture.

Chorus calls went out for dancers at the Copa. At this open call, some of the hundreds of applicants practice their dance steps on the old Villa Vallee stage while others await their turn. By selecting six of the prettiest girls in show business for his glamorous and alluringly beautiful line of girls, including showgirl Hilda Ferguson, namesake of a Ziegfeld beauty, Monte Proser created an ingenious liaison between Broadway and his nightclub. (Photograph by A. Eriss; courtesy of Country Press Inc.)

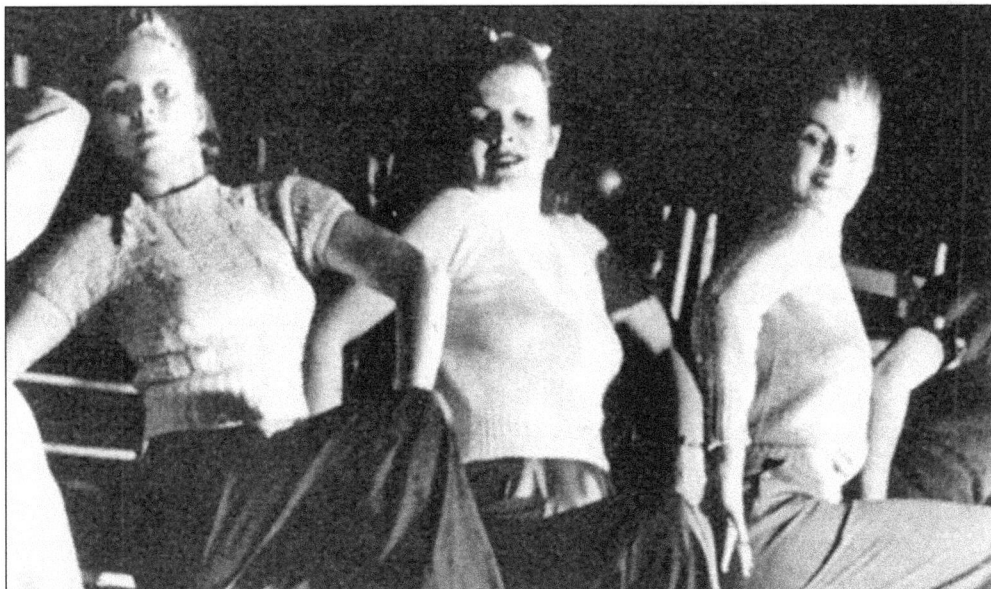

Under the guidance of choreographers Margery (Midge) Fielding and Bob Alton, the girls (from left to right, Doris Greb, Hilda Ferguson, and Jackie Gateley) rehearsed for weeks to perfect their line work, specialties, and—an innovation for a nightclub—individual presentations. They were dubbed the Samba Sirens (later Copa Girls) and became as much a trademark of the Copacabana as the palm trees and the logo of the turban-topped alluring woman. (Photograph by A. Eriss; courtesy of Country Press Inc.)

Samba Siren Rosemary (Rosie) Sankey was one of the first chorus dancers (followed later by Mary Ganly and Virginia Morris) to dash across town after the theater curtain came down from the hit Broadway show *Louisiana Purchase* to be on the Copa floor for the first show at midnight. After the Copa she went on to dance in *By Jupiter*, 1942–1943. (Courtesy of the Harry Ransom Humanities Research Center, the University of Texas at Austin.)

After performing in *Gypsy Blonde*, George White's *Scandals*, *Red, Hot and Blue*, and *You Never Know*, Grace Gillern appeared in the chorus of *Louisiana Purchase* and doubled as a Samba Siren. She went on to marry actor Frank Albertson and enjoyed a highly successful career in Hollywood, returning to Broadway in 1958 as Franklin D. Roosevelt's secretary in *Sunrise at Campobello*. (Photograph by De Mirjian; courtesy of the Harry Ransom Humanities Research Center, the University of Texas at Austin.)

Doris Greb was dancing in *Hold On to Your Hats*, when she was hired for the Copa's first line. She stayed for only a short while and was replaced by Ruth Brady in the second line. (Courtesy of the Harry Ransom Humanities Research Center, the University of Texas at Austin; Bernard of Hollywood Pub/Renaissance Road Inc.)

Jackie Gateley was a dancer in *Streets of Paris* prior to being cast by Al Jolson in the chorus of *Hold On to Your Hats* and doubling as a Samba Siren. (Photograph by De Bellis; courtesy of the Harry Ransom Humanities Research Center, the University of Texas at Austin;.)

Marguerite (Maggie) James had appeared in *Red, Hot and Blue*, *Streets Of Paris*, and *Higher and Higher*, before dancing in *Panama Hattie* and at the Copacabana. Also appearing as dancing girls in *Panama Hattie* were Jane Ball, Lucille Bremer, and June Allyson, all of whom soon would become Samba Sirens. (Photograph by New York Journal-American; courtesy of the Harry Ransom Humanities Research Center, the University of Texas at Austin.)

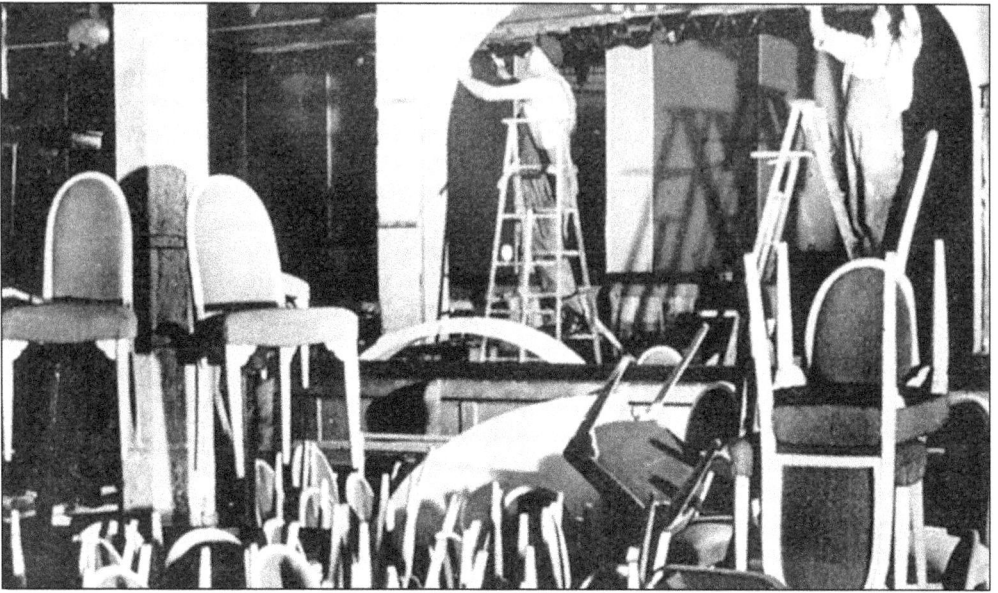

It was a big leap from the stark atmosphere of an old Prohibition club to an up-to-the-minute Latin-American hot spot, but the spectacular transformation was made in less than two months. As demolition workers began removing all traces of the shuttered Villa Vallee, chairs were stacked against large pillars that would be transformed into huge white palm trees with large coconuts and reddish-brown velveteen leaves. The palm trees would become one of the most famous trademarks of the Copacabana. (Photograph by A. Eriss; courtesy of Country Press Inc.)

With no bar in the Prohibition Villa Vallee, designer Clark Robinson decided to locate a bar where the stage had been. His plan included a prominent, long, illuminated mural behind the bar that represented Rio's picturesque harbor by night. A wall-length mirror on the opposite side of the room would reflect the entire space, making the room seem twice its actual size. (Photograph by A. Eriss; courtesy of Country Press Inc.)

The walls, stripped of the old mirrors, were repaired by plasterers then painted white and a vibrant green to give the room a neat, more spacious appearance. (Photograph by A. Eriss; courtesy of Country Press Inc.)

Thick cloth panels were incorporated into the reconstruction of the room, including the entire ceiling, to help reduce the blaring sound of the brass instruments in the band. (Photograph by A. Eriss; courtesy of Country Press Inc.)

Clark Robinson, who had created the South Sea Island décor of Monte Proser's original Beachcomber, ingeniously executed the entrepreneur's vision, or Broadway version, of a splendid, exotic atmosphere. Robinson is shown here evaluating the Brazilian motif that would pervade the strikingly attractive room and create a warm, intimate setting, with mirrored columns, walls, ramps, blue lighting, and maroon furnishings. (Photograph by A. Eriss; courtesy of Country Press Inc.)

The prestigious Pancho and his orchestra, hired to provide the music for the show and dancing along with Fausto Curbelo and his rumba band, rehearsed as electricians and others worked to complete the renovation for the late October opening. (Photograph by A. Eriss; courtesy of Country Press Inc.)

Pedro Pujal, who had worked at the World's Fair Terrace Club, was hired as chef. Dante, who had been in charge of the fair's federal building, was hired as headwaiter to direct food service, assisted by Raymond, who was brought over from the Beachcomber. The rest of the non-entertainment staff of bartenders, busboys, cooks, and waiters, hired and drilled in the fundamentals of food, drink, and professional service, are shown putting the tables in place. (Photograph by A. Eriss; courtesy of Country Press Inc.)

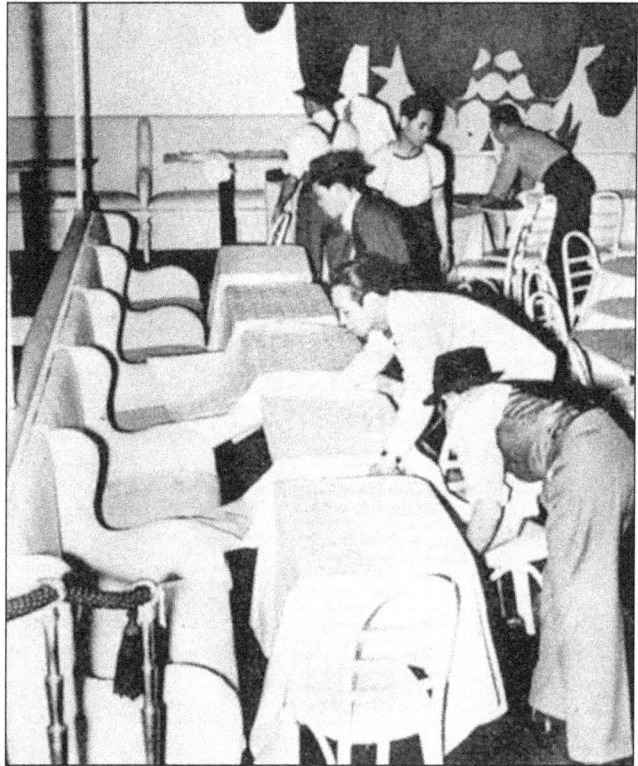

Jack Entratter, formerly of the Stork Club, was hired as managing director. At 25, he was one of the youngest in the business. A familiar figure as the Copa's number one greeter in the early years, Entratter is shown here taking inventory in the Copacabana wine cellar in a 1946 photograph. (Courtesy of Bettmann/Corbis.)

The Copa did not hire big-name stars in the early days. Headliners were the world-famous ballroom dance team of Ramon and Renita, who, in 1935, were featured in the film *Gold Diggers* and named the "King and Queen of Dance" by the *Washington Post*. Authentic Latin-American ingredients were provided by dark, flashy songstress Juanita Juarez, originally from Rio and for a time at La Conga, accompanied by Brazilian "personality kid" Fernando Alvares. Alvares, who married Copa Girls Maju Soares, from Rio, and later Norma Bartlett, was well known for his Portuguese chansons and for emceeing at Rio's Cassino da Urca. Despite the fact that the publicity releases emphasized the huge, white palm trees and a truly sophisticated revue, it was the exceptionally beautiful Copa Girls who regularly brought customers back, in what was described by Walter Winchell as "the best girl show in town." Ramon and Renita are shown here in an undated photograph. (Courtesy of Reni Churchill.)

Two

The Great American Nightclub
1940–1942

The Copacabana Prevue arrived, Wednesday, October 30, 1940, and it was a fabulous, unforgettable night. It was as pulsating and electric as any glamorous, star-studded Broadway premiere. Everyone raved about the lively Latin-American musical rhythms and the ingenious décor, with its attractive palmetto motif and expansive mirrors through which most patrons viewed the show, including those seated at the elevated bar and the banquette perches. (Courtesy of Bettmann/Corbis.)

The Copa brought the intimate revue east of Fifth Avenue, providing a swanky setting where patrons could see first-class entertainment, which was more akin to a full-dress Broadway-style musical production than a nightclub show, eat a full-course dinner, enjoy good music, a full evening of dancing, and drink in the beauty of the Broadway-doubling Samba Sirens and their considerable feminine allure. (Photograph by A. Eriss; courtesy of Country Press Inc.)

There were two shows, midnight and 2:00 a.m., with an original 400-seat capacity. There was no cover charge, but there was a minimum charge of $2 on weekdays and $3 on Saturdays and holidays. Café society favorite El Morocco was the only other club in the $3 minimum bracket; the Diamond Horseshoe, with its elaborate shows only charged $1 and $2; and at Leon and Eddie's, known for its madcap fun, the minimum after 10:00 p.m. was $2. (Courtesy of Lion Match.)

The Copa's Table d'Hôte
DINNER
SERVED TILL 10 P. M.

Hors d'Oeuvres

FILET OF HERRING, SOUR CREAM   HALF GRAPEFRUIT

SALMON APPETIZER   CHERRYSTONE CLAMS COCKTAIL

CHILLED CLAM, TOMATO, VEGETABLE OR GRAPEFRUIT JUICE

CHILLED HALF CANTALOUPE

Potages

POTAGE MALAKOFF   ONION SOUP

COLD JELLY MADRILENE

Entrees

FRIED FILET OF SOLE, TARTAR SAUCE	2.75
GRILLED FRESH SEA TROUT, JEANNE D'ARC	3.00
SPRING CHICKEN EN COCOTTE, CHASSEUR (Half)	3.50
MIGNONETTE OF MILK FED VEAL POELE, A L'ESTRAGON	3.50
BRAISED LONG ISLAND DUCKLING, DANOISE	3.75
BROILED LOIN OF LAMB WITH KIDNEY, ANGLAISE	3.50
CHINESE: SUB GUM CHICKEN CHOP SUEY WITH GREEN PEPPERS, MUSHROOMS AND ALMONDS	3.25
COLD: ROAST PRIME RIBS OF BEEF WITH POTATO SALAD AND STRING BEANS	4.25

Legumes

BUTTERED GREEN PEAS   POMME VOISIN

MIXED GREEN SALAD

Desserts

FRUIT COMPOTE   MOCCA CAKE   FROZEN ECLAIR

HALF GRAPEFRUIT SEEDLESS   RASPBERRY SHERBET

CHOCOLATE, STRAWBERRY OR VANILLA ICE CREAM

ROQUEFORT OR CAMEMBERT CHEESE

COFFEE, TEA OR MILK

Thursday, July 11, 1946

Monte Proser's
COPACABANA
10 EAST 60th   NEW YORK

All prices are out ceiling prices or below. By O.P.A. regulation our ceilings are based upon
our highest prices from April 4 to 10, 1943, inclusive. Our menus or price lists for that week
are available for your inspection.

The Copacabana was operated as a supper club, with doors opening at 9 p.m. Dinners were $2 and up; a drink, 75¢. The menu originally reflected the Latin-American theme, with Brazilian dishes, but also featured and became famous for its Oriental cuisine. The floor staff of maitre d's, captains, waiters, and busboys were well-trained, wore tuxedoes or uniforms, and behaved with impeccably professional (not flamboyant) decorum, keeping the service as excellent as the food. An advertising flyer later would boast: "The Copa is known as the one nightclub in New York City, where the old phrase 'nightclub food,' does not apply. Smart New Yorkers are aware that the Copa's food is the equal of that served at the top eating places of this food-conscious town. We wish that we could take every one of you on a tour of these truly fabulous kitchens where the Copa food is prepared. They are huge, exciting, filled with food and drink of the finest quality, and all prepared by master chefs." (Courtesy of Copacabana/John Juliano.)

Fernando Alvares is shown singing while six lovely Samba Sirens rumba in their magnificent, exotic costumes individually designed by Bea Ammidown and executed by Brooks, a costume shop for all the Broadway shows. From the beginning, the Copacabana was known for first-rate talent and both stunningly beautiful girls and costumes. (Photograph by A. Eriss; courtesy of Country Press Inc.)

A top-notch pianist who played in the Xavier Cugat Orchestra, Fausto Curbelo formed his own orchestra that became one of the most sought-after of the day. In addition to providing first-rate Latin music for the first Copa shows, he was also establishing a reputation for his song-compositions, like "The Thrill of a New Romance" (1939) and "The Girl with the Spanish Drawl" (1940).

The Copacabana was hailed as New York's "No. 1 nitery click" and the latest jewel in Monte Proser's string of successful nightclubs. The Copa's gross of $14,000 was the highest among nightclubs in New York City within only a month of its opening. The Copacabana was on its way to national fame and a reputation as the Great American Nightclub. (Courtesy of Frank Driggs.)

The Copa's second show, which opened January 27, 1941, was considered to be an innovative departure for a nightclub anywhere as one of its featured acts was a ballet dancer, Patricia Bowman, shown here in a 1937 photograph. She was known for her Broadway appearances in *Ziegfeld Follies of 1934*, *Calling All Stars*, *Virginia*, and in the film, *Okay for Sound*, and later, the operetta *Rhapsody* and the *Patricia Bowman Show* (1951) television series. (Courtesy of AP Images.)

Low-pitched, liquid-voiced Elvira Rios, shown here in a 1938 photograph, was already a favorite of radio listeners and filmgoers when she was hired by the Copa and silenced a well-filled room with her soft, throbbing Mexican songs. Holdovers were Fernando Alvares and songstress Juanita Juarez, who also fronted for her husband's Frank Marti's Rumba Band, which, along with Nat Brandwynne's Orchestra, came aboard at this time and began their long associations with the Copacabana. (Courtesy of AP Images.)

In early March 1941, torch singer Bernice Parks, shown here in a 1943 photograph, formerly a vocalist with the Russ Morgan Orchestra, was headlining at the Copacabana and doubling in the new stage show at the Paramount. The new roster also featured a popular dance team of the day, Johnny Mack and Lyda Sue. A third show was added at 8:00 p.m. (Courtesy of AP Images.)

Samba Sirens Hilda Ferguson and Ruth Brady were replaced by *Panama Hattie* dancing girls Jane Ball and Lucille Bremer, who went on to make her MGM film debut with Judy Garland in *Meet Me in St. Louis*. Bremer is probably best remembered for her talent as a dancer and partner with Fred Astaire in *Yolanda and the Thief* and *Ziegfeld Follies*, shown here. (Courtesy of Culver Pictures.)

All-American blonde Jane Ball, who married Copa creator Monte Proser in 1945, left the Copa line and signed with Twentieth Century-Fox, starring in *Winged Victory*, shown here (center), *Keys of the Kingdom*, both released in 1944, and *Forever Amber*, her final film appearance. (Courtesy of Twentieth Century-Fox.)

Irene Vernon, who roomed with Lucille Bremer when they were among the first girls to be part of the Copacabana Revue at Piping Rock, which was the Copa's counterpart operation on the outskirts of Saratoga, was also signed by MGM. Pictured at a party thrown for the Goldwyn Girls are, from left to right, Jackie Jordan, Irene Vernon, Mary Brewer, Danny Kaye, Karen Gaylord, Sue Casey, Georgia Lange, Eve Arden, and Mary Ellen Gleason. (Photograph by Merv Watson; courtesy of Culver Pictures.)

One of the best-known of all the Copa Girls was vivacious, petite June Allyson, shown here in an undated photograph. While performing as a chorus girl in *Panama Hattie* and then *Best Foot Forward*, she doubled at the Copacabana. She was signed by MGM and went on to host the *June Allyson Show*. Later she starred in the *Incredible Hulk* television series and *Three and a Date* Movie-of-the-Week, with former Copa Girl Edna Ryan as her understudy for both shows. (Courtesy of AP Images.)

Monte Proser closed down for the hot summer months and shifted the entire staff to luxuriant Piping Rock, shown here, for the August racing and social season. The Saratoga facility was much larger than the Copa and was known as a premier gambling resort for organized crime and New York society. Mafia kingpin Meyer Lansky used the cover of the existing restaurant to hide the illegal gambling casino operation from the law. (Courtesy of George S. Bolster Collection at the Saratoga Springs History Museum.)

Big-name entertainers like Sophie Tucker and Joe E. Lewis were hired for the no-expense-spared presentations. A new show was put together, with new production numbers, new costumes, and Copacabana girls chosen at random from among those free for the six-to-eight-week season. (Courtesy of Ed Hertel.)

Mafia boss Frank Costello, shown here in a downtown Manhattan office building, was, along with New Jersey club operator Joe Adonis, brought into Piping Rock by Meyer Lansky, who used a local town official's name on the license to front the gaming operation. Likewise Monte Proser's name was put on the Copacabana license and was listed as president and majority shareholder of record, but other partners were Jules Podell, his brother-in-law Sidney Robinson, and Frank Costello. The illusion that the Copa was other than mob-controlled was spread by columnists like Walter Winchell, who described the club as "Monte Proser's Copacabana." Several years later the licensing bureau under Mayor Fiorello La Guardia proposed to refuse renewal of the Copcabana's cabaret license on the grounds that some of the club's owners had gambling associations. Costello also would appear in early 1951 before Sen. Estes Kefauver's nationally televised Senate Crime Investigating Committee, regarding his ties to organized crime, but he would successfully withstand efforts by the city prosecutor to testify on the ownership of the Copacabana. (Courtesy of AP Images.)

Simultaneous to shifting the Copa staff to Saratoga, Monte Proser presented a Copacabana Revue at the newly-decorated, renowned Terrace Room at the Hotel New Yorker, with Johnny Long and his orchestra, featuring vocalists Helen Young and Bob Houston. (Courtesy of E. C. Kropp.)

After suffering permanent damage to his right hand, young Johnny Long learned to play the violin left-handed, making him unique among headliners. Long and his orchestra's sweet, musical sound was popular with the ballroom dance crowd and they played in some of the best hotels in the country. (Courtesy of AP Images.)

The successful engagement at the Hotel New Yorker led to the booking by Interstate Theatres of a Copacabana Revue headed by one of the top Latin bandleaders of the day, Colombian-born Carlos Molina and his orchestra, and included six Samba Sirens, soprano Rosita Rios (shown here), Estelle and Le Roy, Tito Coral, and Victoria Cordona. They were booked for shows in Houston, San Antonio, Dallas, Fort Worth, and Austin, with negotiations underway for October and Clyde McCoy bookings set for November 1941. These productions were so well received that Proser's Copacabana Revue from New York remained an intact road show that played in nightclubs around the country. The revues were touted as the same colorful, top-notch floor show that was presented at New York's Copacabana, now a touring, intact unit that could be seen nationwide in deluxe motion picture houses, hotels, and niteries. (Courtesy of AP Images.)

A new personality, Aurora, younger sister of the famous Carmen Miranda, reopened the Copacabana, October 2, 1941, with a vibrant Cariocan revue. Charles Baum and his orchestra, known for their renditions of popular songs, like "Deep Purple," replaced Nat Brandwynne, who went to Ciro's in Hollywood.

Samba sessions were growing, contrary to an abortive effort by nightclubs in the late 1930s to make the South American dance catch on. Maestro Frank Marti rendered orchestral arrangements of the newly introduced "Tico Tico No Fuba," and other songs, and was largely responsible for making the samba a successful Copacabana innovation and another one of its trademarks.

41

DON   MAXINE
LOPER & BARRAT
AT
MONTE PROSER'S COPACABANA
10 EAST 60TH NEW YORK PL 8-1060

Sharing top billing with Aurora (Miranda) of the 1941 fall opening show was the sleek dance team of Don Loper (later a successful Hollywood couturier) and Maxine Barrat, who performed the samba, which also typified the native Brazilian Copa Little Shows. Loper and Barrat were directly responsible for making the samba the nightly highlight of the current show and the Copacabana getting credit for its widespread popularity in the early 1940s. During a six-month engagement at Rio's Copacabana district casinos, hotel employees had brought them the sheet music of many native Brazilian songs, including "Tico Tico No Fuba." When approached by music publishers at the Copacabana, they freely gave the song to them—at no charge—and lost out on any of its big money-making potential. Their innovative integration of native steps into their Copa presentation contrasted with the typical glossy ballroom styles of other café performers, and both their choreography and dancing received rave reviews. (Courtesy of Maxine Barrat Carter.)

On the advice of his William Morris press agents and in a move to counter mounting competition from other nightclubs, Monte Proser inaugurated a big-name policy. The Copacabana's first anniversary show, October 31, 1941, was headlined by Gertrude Niesen, who was a musical comedy and radio star of the 1930s. Also underway were negotiations to bring in Joe E. Lewis as the first talking comic ever to play the Copa.

Filipino concert-opera songstress Enya Gonzalez headlined the next show in early December 1941, with staging by Billy Reed. A former vaudeville and Broadway hoofer, Billy Reed was Monte Proser's dance director and assistant producer for a number of the early shows. After serving in the U.S. Navy during World War II he opened his famed Little Club, a favorite of show people, where he is shown toasting actress Denise Darcel in an undated photograph. (Courtesy of Culver Pictures.)

When the Japanese unleashed their horrific air attack on the United States military base at Pearl Harbor the morning of December 7, 1941, the nation was stunned. The challenging and common goal of defeating the enemies, Germany and Japan, came to be known as the War Effort, and the Copacabana would do its part in the years to come. The entertainment industry in general provided a respite from war weariness, and flashy, elaborate floor shows and paradoxical gaiety abounded in nightclubs. Copa Girls donated their time as USO club hostesses at the popular Stage Door Canteen and as models for clothing drives and other publicity campaigns. On October 12, 1944, the Copa played host to more than 500 wounded veterans who were recuperating at St. Albans Naval Hospital. One of the lovely Copa Girls is shown at the event with Claude Bocklaman (left), United States Naval Reserve, of Jasper, Indiana, and Harold Milson, United States Naval Reserve, of Waterbury, Connecticut. (Courtesy of Bettmann/Corbis.)

Monte Proser
PRESENTS

JOE E. LEWIS

AUSTIN MACK at the Piano

in Bob Wright and Chet Forrest's New Copa Revue

HERMANOS WILLIAMS TRIO

BARRY SISTERS • LARRY BROOKS • DON LIBERTO

WINN SEELEY • THE SAMBA SIRENS

SONNY KENDIS & HIS ORCH.

FRANK MARTI's SAMBA BAND

FOR DINNER AT 8 – Then at 12 – Again at 2

Monte Proser's
COPACABANA

10 EAST 60TH   PLaza 8-1060

Joe E. Lewis, the garrulous, gravelly-voiced, beloved crown prince of comedy and one of the Copa's most popular performers throughout its glory years, made his premiere appearance January 9, 1942. It was Monte Proser, who, as a publicity agent for the 1937 musical in which Lewis had a part, *Right This Way*, came up with the idea to add an *E* to his name to distinguish him from the famous prize fighter Joe Lewis. Headliner Joe E. Lewis skyrocketed business at the fledgling club at 10 East 60th Street and played an unprecedented total of 38 weeks in two stints. The fractional advertisement shown here appeared in a November 1943 entertainment publication.

The crowning touch of fashion in the 1940s was the hat. The latest fashions, including headgear, were mirrored in the ensembles of the Copa's Samba Sirens and performers. Civilians and men of the armed forces are shown on the crowded sidewalks of New York's Fifth Avenue in a February 21, 1943, photograph. (Courtesy of AP Images.)

The spotlight in February 1942 was on the multitalented Don Loper, who, in addition to selecting the Samba Sirens, directing, choreographing, and performing, designed every garment and headpiece worn in the Copa's new, critically-acclaimed show *Flying Down to Rio–and Back*. Don Loper and Maxine Barrat (center) are shown relaxing with two Samba Sirens in a 1942 photograph. (Courtesy of AP Images.)

With the return of Joe E. Lewis, who came in to start off every new fall season, the Copacabana reopened October 1, 1942, after a summer closing. The club's third year got off to a dynamite start, picking up where Joe E. Lewis, now doubling at Loew's State Theater, left off when the room closed in June. The Copa's fine atmosphere was now even more superb with a refurbishing and enlargement job done while the Copa staff sojourned in upstate New York. From the original seating capacity of 400 it went to 550 in its second year, and now, by building out the terraces, as seen in this photograph, Monte Proser was able to squeeze in 670 at the tables, plus another 50 or so at the bar. The Copacabana then had the biggest nightclub capacity on the East Side and one of the biggest in New York City. (Courtesy of Frank Driggs.)

Don Loper staged the production and designed the outstanding costumes in this fine initial show. Other highlights included the Berry Brothers; Connie Russell; suave Latin singer and original emcee, holdover Fernando Alvares; and ballroom dancer Pierre D'Angelo. Peppery Latin performer Olga San Juan, shown in an undated photograph, was used as an incidental touch in a couple of numbers with the Samba Sirens. (Courtesy of Brendan O'Brien.)

The show was praised for hitting a high standard musically, with two-year-holdover Frank Marti providing rumbas, congas, and sambas while bandleader Ted Straeter supplied outstanding playing for the show and fox trots. Straeter, shown here, was well known for his independent, single-entity society band that basically catered to a generation that just simply wanted to dance. (Courtesy of Harriet Wright.)

Three

EVERYTHING IS COPASETIC
1943–1944

Coined by Bill "Bojangles" Robinson back in his early Richmond days, the term "copasetic" meant that everything was better than all right. It described the ambiance of the Copacabana, the mood, and the feeling that everything was fine and dandy, even as war news dominated headlines. A wartime craving for fun and refuge abounded, resulting in a record-breaking season for nightclubs across America; in fact, many were enjoying the greatest boom in their history. Americans had been at war for two years and many men and women, including entertainers, were doing their part at home and at the front. Defense workers, who were making big money, were spending freely in New York's watering holes and hospitality was being extended to men in uniform. Sophie Tucker, "Last of the Red Hot Mamas," is shown here belting out her signature song, "Some of These Days," to a wartime 1940s audience at the Copacabana, April 7, 1944. (Courtesy of AP Images.)

The new Copa show in March 1943, with lovable, perennial favorite Jimmy Durante headlining for the first time, was described in the trade papers as "very copasetic." Opening night was completely sold out and Friday's gross was the best Friday, in money, in the history of the Copa to date. The Jimmy Durante of "Inka Dinka Doo" fame, who would soon be touted as America's number one clown, had Monte Proser to thank for his comeback when his personal life was mired with tragedy and Hollywood had decided he was through. With his wife Jeanne terminally ill, he found solace in returning after a 12-year hiatus to the nightclub floor at the Copacabana, where he was such a hit that he was held over for 14 weeks. Durante was a steady, always funny comedian, who exemplified the durability of a select few who were able to maintain a level of consistency and attract business year after year, making him as popular in 1943 as he was in the old Prohibition days. He is shown in his Copacabana dressing room with seven Copa lovelies in a 1952 photograph.

Special mention was made of the show's effective staging by Larry Ceballos (who later staged the musical numbers for the film *Copacabana*) as well as the clothes and hats by Walter Florell, whose work at the Copa propelled his reputation as a surefire production artisan. Walter Florell became known for his elaborations on the portentous turban, popularized by Carmen Miranda, and as a custom millinery designer. He is shown here with one of his models, Wendy Russell, in a 1947 photograph. (Courtesy of AP Images.)

In addition to establishing a reputation for helping out performers who had fallen on hard times, Monte Proser was also credited with discovering some of the big names in entertainment, like former Canonsburg, Pennsylvania, barber Perry Como, who is shown here. As the story goes, Proser happened to turn on the radio one day, heard Como's voice, phoned the station, and booked Como sight unseen for his first Copa appearance in spring 1943.

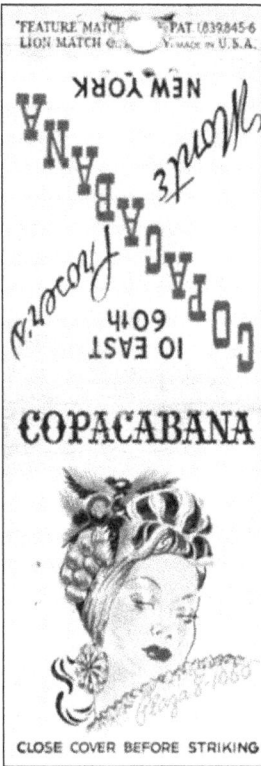

From its inception, Monte Proser had envisioned the Copacabana as an escapist's paradise, where people would flock for the transient thrill of rubbing elbows with the rich and famous. His entrepreneurial talent also played out in the creation of the turban-topped alluring woman logo, which successfully projected his vision. A Copacabana advertising matchbook cover with original logo is shown here. (Courtesy of Lion Match.)

While dancing in the Copa line in 1943, beautiful Emily Jewell captivated Monte Proser with her stunning looks. He told artist Wesley Morse that this was the look he wanted for the Copacabana logo and commissioned him to update it based on her likeness. The Copacabana advertising postcard remained unchanged throughout the years except for the increases in minimum charges. A postcard with the revised (Emily Jewell) logo is shown here. (Courtesy of Copacabana/John Juliano.)

In 1943, an upstairs cocktail room, where "something new and beautiful has been added," was attracting attention and catching overflow business. The new cocktail bar offered continuous entertainment from "COCKTAIL TIME till the Witching Hours," initially presenting Peppy De Albrew along with featured acts, like Los Andrini, who also played the main room downstairs. Copacabana matchbooks advertising the new Copa lounge are shown here with original logo (left), and revised logo. (Left, courtesy of Lion Match; right, courtesy of Diamond Match.)

In time the Copa lounge became not only a favorite watering hole for regular customers, celebrities, and wiseguys, but also a spot for performers to showcase their acts. Popular acts included the Nat Cole Trio, Lena Horne, and Wayne Newton, who played there for 19 weeks with a band, and others. Nat Cole Trio members are, from left to right, Oscar Moore (guitar), Wesley Prince (double bass), and Nat King Cole (piano), in a 1940 photograph.

In Monte Proser's mind it was beauty that was principal to a successful nightclub production, whether it be the musical score, the arrangements, the costumes, the girls, or even the performers, whenever possible. Beyond beauty, he looked for personality, talent, intelligence, and a feminine charm whenever he picked a girl for the line. Every season, since theatrical producer Florenz Ziegfeld first started glorifying showgirls, a different nightclub claimed to have the most beautiful, statuesque, and full-bosomed line of girls in New York. Now the Copa boasted this claim. Monte Proser's impeccable taste and talent for picking girls was evidenced in the club's first half-dozen years, when almost 60 girls were taken right off the floor by movie scouts. Among those in the early years for whom the Copacabana was a springboard to fame were June Allyson, Lucille Bremer, Adele Jergens, Martha Stewart, Mary Elliott, Marylin Johnson, Adele Mara, Jane Ball, and Joanne Marshall (later Dru). Marshall went from dancing in *Hold On to Your Hats* to the Copa line and on to Hollywood. She is shown with Van Johnson in one of her classic Western roles in *The Siege at Red River*. (Courtesy of Twentieth Century-Fox.)

Monte Proser liked ambitious girls, and many Copa Girls pursued modeling or took acting or singing lessons while employed by the club. Aspiring young vocalist Janis Paige got her big break when she was spotted by some George Abbott scouts while appearing on the Joe E. Lewis bill at the Copa. She was signed for Broadway's Tony Award-winning musical comedy, *Pajama Game*, and went on to Hollywood and a memorable part in *Silk Stockings* (shown here) and later appeared on numerous television shows. (*Silk Stockings* © Turner Entertainment Company. A Warner Bros. Entertainment Company. All rights reserved.)

The Copa Girls were always dazzlingly attired from head to toe with stunning creations by top designers like Bea Ammidown, Don Loper, Miles White, Ted Shore, Billy Livingston, Sal Anthony, Alvin Colt, and Michi. Their exotic costumes and magnificent gowns, executed by Mme Berthe, made the Copa Girls the best-dressed showgirls in town. Copa Girl Diane Milne is seen in a 1949 photograph wearing mink accessories and standing next to the rack of gowns, which were meticulously handled and covered for storage in the girls' dressing room. (Courtesy of Terri Stevens Norbeck.)

Monte Proser's stamp on a girl gave her an immediate beauty. His touch was magic. On the night she first stepped out onto the floor, she became famous. She was a Copa Girl. She was a vision of loveliness and the American dream girl, the stage-door Johnny's lush lovely, who was showered with champagne, jewels, and furs. She was a newspaper boy's focus of attention and every man's object of desire. Samba Siren Lucille Bremer, who became a star of classic musicals, is shown in a 1944 photograph. (Courtesy of AP Images.)

The spectacularly beautiful Copa Girls were one of the most successful and popular of the many ideas that Monte Proser brought to the New York nightclub scene. They brought in the crowds, and they were the talk of the town. They were wined, dined, invited everywhere, and written up daily in the gossip columns. Copa Girl Norma Bartlett is shown backstage in the girls' dressing room in a 1949 photograph. (Courtesy of Terri Stevens Norbeck.)

The basic criteria required by Monte Proser were girls between the ages of 18 and 21, and an average size of five feet, and five or six inches, not the over-sized showgirls sought by other nightclub producers. Hair color was incidental, but there was usually a balance between blondes and brunettes. Salary was $50 to $75 a week in the 1940s and $100 in the 1950s. Among Monte Proser's sources when scouting for girls were Broadway shows; Atlantic City's beauty pageants, where he found Pat Patrick (Miss Wisconsin), Ruth Brady (Miss Brooklyn), and Lucille Casey (Miss Newark); famous show biz hangouts, like the Astor Hotel pharmacy-coffee shop and the coffee counter at Hanson's (near the Roxy) drugstore; and, even bus stations, which were scouted for potential discoveries. The girls rehearsing at the Copa are, from left to right, Mary Elliott, Betty De Witt, Virginia Wilson (dancing), Ruth Brady, and unidentified. (Courtesy of Bettmann/Corbis.)

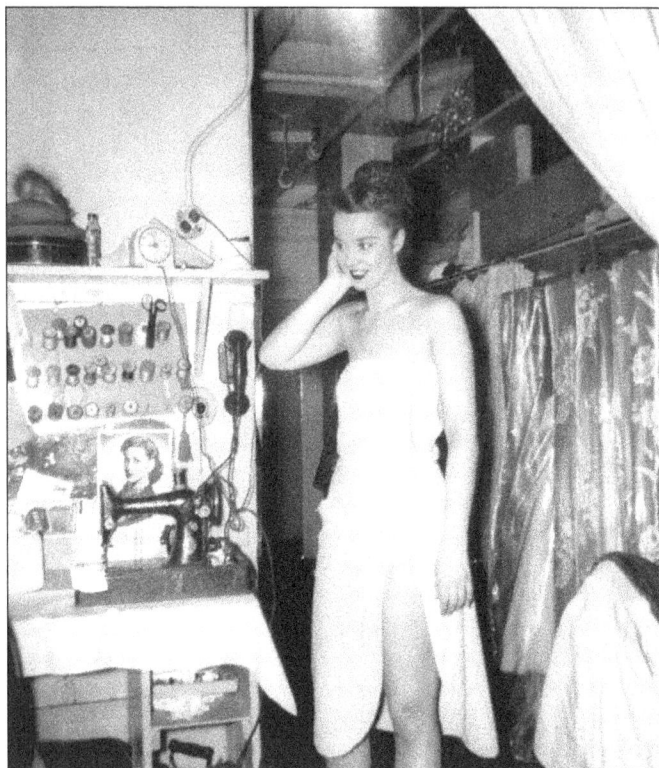

The Copa Girls were known for their trademark, upswept hairdos, which contributed to their overall well-groomed look. They wore little make-up. They were the framework for the show and the epitome of beauty and exclusivity. Diane Milne is shown in the Copa Girls' dressing room in a 1949 photograph. (Courtesy of Terri Stevens Norbeck.)

Petite, former ballerina Marion Alexander was the Copacabana wardrobe mistress for many years. She is shown sitting at her sewing table in the Copa Girls' dressing room in this 1949 photograph. The photograph behind the sewing machine is of one of her favorite Copa performers, comedienne Jean Carroll. (Courtesy of Terri Stevens Norbeck.)

The new Winter Revue of December 1943, starring Jimmy Durante with Eddie Jackson and Jack Roth, was staged by a young, unknown dancer-choreographer named Virgil Douglas (Doug) Coudy, whose extraordinary talent in directing the production numbers and dances was immediately recognized and received national attention. By the next show he was fully credited for producing the show, marking the beginning of his position as Copacabana producer, a position that he held for the next 30 years. Coudy became the central figure in the behind-the-scenes operation of the club. He not only directed the floor shows, but ran the whole show, booking production numbers and main acts, contracting for music, and working lights and sound as well as announcing and choreographing. As importantly, he had the responsibility of one of the mainstays—and biggest draws—of the Copacabana, the girls. Coudy became their director, producer, friend, father figure, and above all else, creator. He is shown backstage at the Copacabana with Copa Girl Diane Milne (center), and production singer Terri Stevens in a 1949 photograph. (Courtesy of Terri Stevens Norbeck.)

The Copa shows were written, directed, and produced like Broadway musicals, with the Copa Girls in rehearsal for four to six weeks. Audition calls for a new group of girls went out every time the production was changed, which was four times a year. Hundreds of girls turned out for the auditions, but only a select few were chosen. Copa bosses looked for a beautiful figure, bone structure, widely-spaced eyes, and a saucy, upturned nose, and, producer Doug Coudy wanted to see how they moved. Then he would begin from scratch, teaching them the routines. He would turn them into Copa Girls, like Barbara Feldon, shown here in a 1965 photograph. (Courtesy of AP Images.)

Doug Coudy inspired and encouraged the girls to develop their individual talents, and he groomed and molded each one into a poised, confident, and beautiful woman. Statuesque Copa Girl Edna Ryan, who had been a dancing girl along with Lillian Moore on Broadway in *Follow the Girls*, is shown with Jonathan Lucas performing in a 1949 Copa show production number. (Courtesy of Edna Ryan Murcott.)

Janice Rule, another Copa Girl who achieved star status, began dancing professionally, first in Chicago, then in New York at the Copacabana and in several Broadway musicals. She made her acting debut in the 1951 film version of the Broadway hit *Goodbye, My Fancy*. In the decades that followed, she worked constantly in theater, features, and television. She is shown here with her husband Ben Gazzara in a December 17, 1961, photograph. (Courtesy of Bettmann/Corbis.)

*Sincerely
Shep Fields*

A newly air-conditioned Copacabana remained open throughout the summer of 1944, with a hot weather revue that inaugurated a name-band policy, whereby the sweet sound of a society band would alternate with Frank Marti's Latin rhythms. Also new was a full WOR-Mutual Radio wire that would bring the Copa's musical presentations into the homes of American families everywhere. Shep Fields, the first of the Copa's society bandleaders, is shown here in an undated photograph.

The fall 1944 show continued the Copa's newly established name-band policy, now with the Abe Lyman Orchestra playing for dancing and Joel Herron's orchestra playing for the show. The new lineup was headed by Joe E. Lewis, and included ballerina Marilyn Hightower, dancer Betty Ann Nyman, former band vocalist Martha Stewart, and singer Johnny Johnston, shown here with his wife Kathryn Grayson and Danny Thomas (center) at a 1948 Martin Block cocktail party. (Photograph by Charles Rhodes; courtesy of Culver Pictures.)

This show was written by Eddie De Lange and Joe Myrow, staged by Doug Coudy, produced by Al Siegel, and costumed by Ted Shore. Joe E. Lewis is shown in a November 27, 1944, photograph as Santa Claus giving gifts to the Copa Girls to send to their girl service friends overseas. From left to right, they are (first row) Ruth Starr and Mara Williams; (second row) Suzanne Graves, Randi Robson, Patsi Mahar, Joe E. Lewis, Mary Mullen, Doris Sands, and Ronan York. (Courtesy of AP Images.)

Four

THOSE WERE THE DAYS
1944–1953

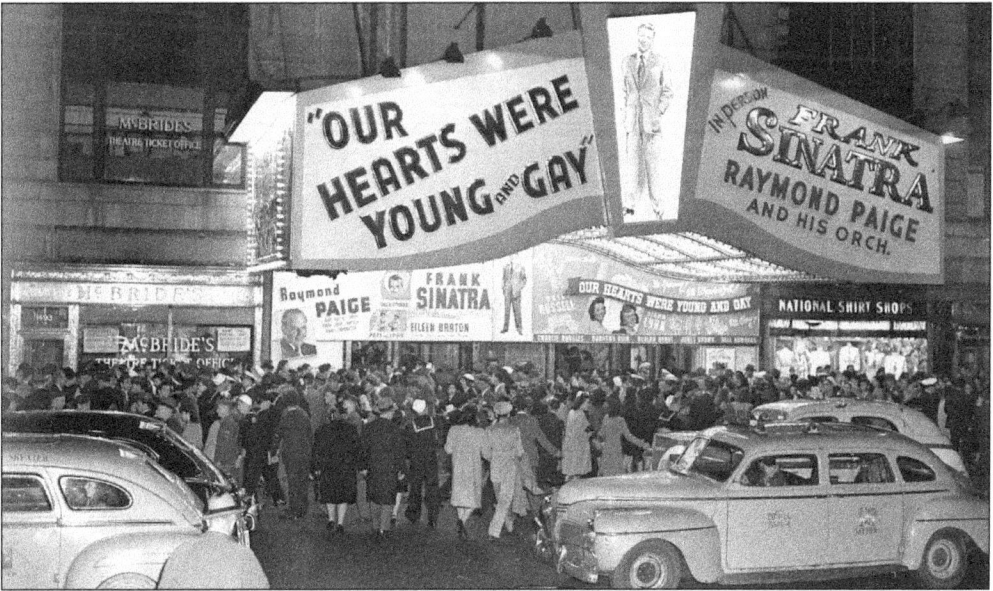

At the beginning of the decade Wurlitzer jukeboxes played hit show tunes, country music, and swing at 5¢ a song, and dancers called hepcats jitterbugged to big-band music. By 1944, the top records included five vocal disks, compared to the previous year, when there were none. Music trends were changing. The stage was now set for the likes of Francis Albert (Frank) Sinatra. The Paramount booking of the "Voice That Thrills Millions" on Columbus Day 1944 persuaded all skeptics that Frank Sinatra was the biggest name in show business. The event was pandemonium and the news media declared it the "Columbus Day Riot at the Paramount." The following day, a school holiday, was even more chaotic as tens of thousands of youngsters lined up for blocks, jamming Times Square, and making it impassable to cars and pedestrians. (Courtesy of AP Images.)

In a triumphant comeback, headliner Jane Froman took her first steps without a cane since she was left crippled following a 1943 plane crash en route to entertain troops in Europe. She came onto the Copa floor during a blackout, standing on a platform in front of a piano, wearing a voluminous skirt. She is joined on the Copa floor by one of her many armed-services fans, an unidentified U.S. Navy warrant officer, in a February 2, 1945, photograph. (Courtesy of AP Images.)

General manager Jack Entratter is shown reading an announcement of employee dismissals due to a wartime midnight curfew at a meeting in the club on February 25, 1945. The Copa employed 250 to 300 people with a $20,000 weekly payroll, including the famous dance team of Tony and Sally De Marco (seated at table, right). The Copa lounge, which remained open, continued to do more business than ever. (Courtesy of AP Images.)

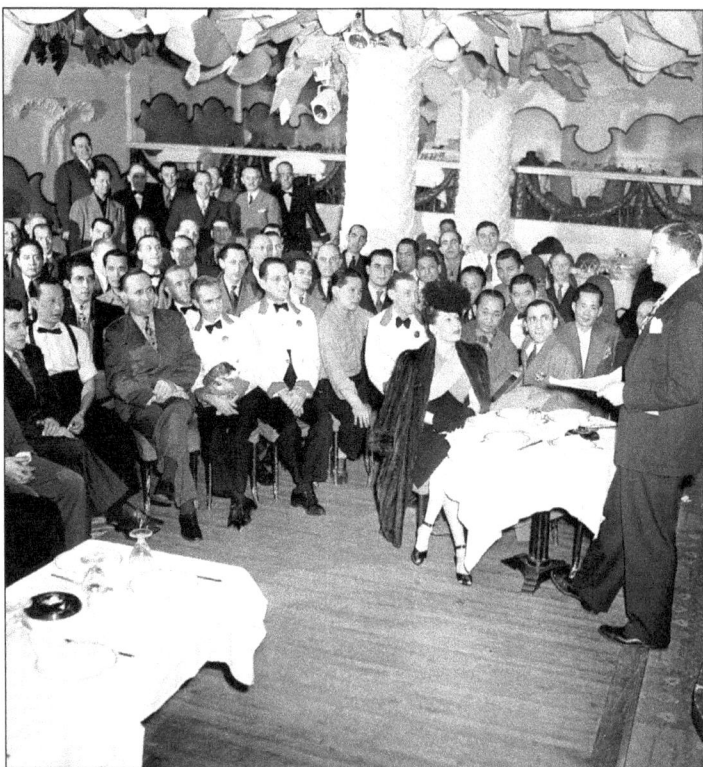

Following the victory in Europe in May 1945, the midnight curfew was lifted. Other nightclubs with entertainment resumed the old schedule of three shows a night, much to the dismay of most of the acts. So accustomed had the performers been to the leisure provided when only two shows were required that they balked at a third show. To this day, many entertainers contract for only two shows nightly—a throwback to the curfew—except on Saturdays, and some of the big-name stars insist on only one show in some of the more prestigious venues, such as hotel supper clubs. By 1946, Jerry Lester, who was very successful with an explosive comedy act, had developed a quieter, even funnier style and quipped, "The things I do for a lousy fortune!"

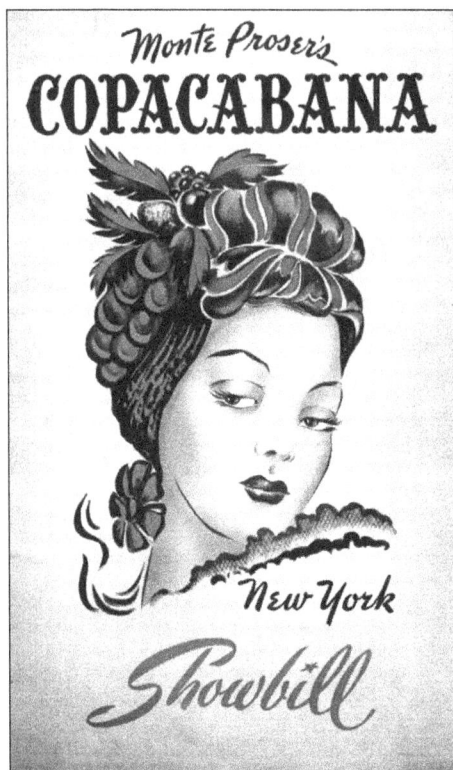

Comedian Jerry Lester started off 1946 in Doug Coudy's New Copa Revue, with dancers Chandra-Kaly and Marina, and singer Jack Leonard, who was making his first nightclub appearance after five years in the U.S. Army. The full cast and credits were listed in the introductory issue of *Showbill*, which was distributed to patrons of 16 New York supper clubs.

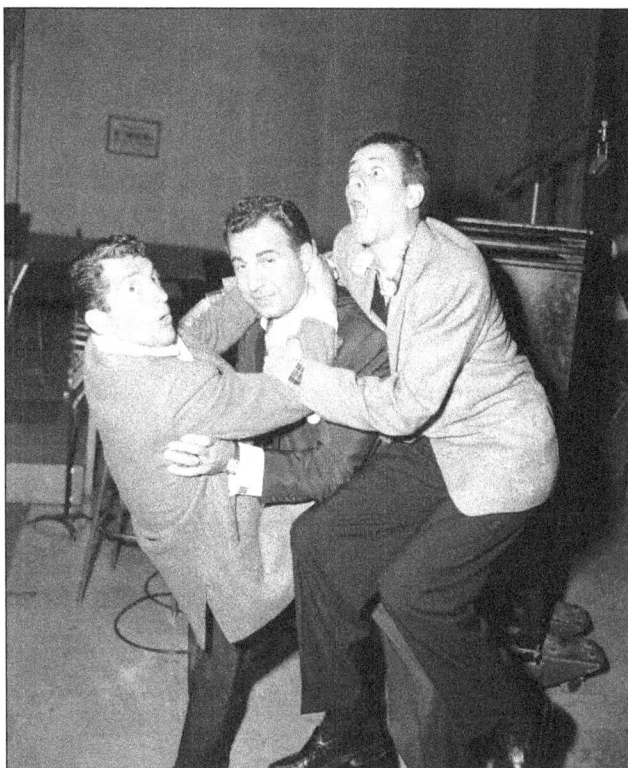

After hearing Dick Stabile and his orchestra open for Frank Sinatra at the Waldorf, Monte Proser hired him to come in as the house band for the Jerry Lester show, alternating on the dance numbers with the Chavez Rumba Band. Dick Stabile's orchestra went on to attain notoriety at Slapsy Maxie's in Hollywood and later, as musical accompaniment to Dean Martin and Jerry Lewis, who are shown clowning with the orchestra leader in a 1952 photograph. (Courtesy of AP Images.)

Romantic balladeer Jack Leonard, one of the late 1930s top male vocalists with the Tommy Dorsey band, was a featured act in the Jerry Lester show. The popular crooner is shown with his new bride, former Copa Girl Edna Ryan, in a July 29, 1948, photograph. (Courtesy of AP Images.)

Pretty blonde production singer Martha Stewart first met and started dating Joe E. Lewis when both were performing in the 1944 fall revue. After the show she was signed by Twentieth Century-Fox and left for Hollywood. Movie starlet Martha Stewart and nightclub entertainer Joe E. Lewis are shown attending their much-celebrated wedding in Miami Beach on March 31, 1946. (Courtesy of AP Images.)

On the April 1946 bill with headliner Jane Froman was Jan Murray, who had been resident comedian at Leon and Eddie's prior to the war. After his discharge, he got back into the business and was catapulted to national fame by his appearance at La Martinique the previous season. While working at the Copacabana he met his beautiful, blonde, future wife, Toni Kelly, who was dancing in the line of girls. (Courtesy of AP Images.)

As a celebrity hangout it was commonplace to see the top names in show business in the Copa audience. Opening nights, in particular, were always pulsating and electric. There was a glamour and excitement about the Copa that did not exist in any other club in America. Dinah Shore is shown seated at a table at the Copa with her husband, actor George Montgomery (left), and Columbia Records head Mannie Sacks, with *Variety*'s Bernie Woods standing behind them, in an undated photograph. (Courtesy of Culver Pictures.)

In 1944, Julie Wilson, shown here in an undated photograph, segued from the dancing line at the Latin Quarter to the Copa. She then worked as a solo act, toured with a Copa-USO show in Europe, and ended up back at the Copa as a production singer. She introduced "They've Got an Awful Lot of Coffee in Brazil" providing an opportunity for some fortunate Copa patrons to hear it performed live in May 1946 before it became a best-selling record for Frank Sinatra later that year. (Courtesy of AP Images.)

At that time motion picture houses offered stage shows with entertainment, from popular orchestras and specialty artists to vaudeville and variety revues. The theaters were open before 1:00 p.m. for the "early-bird" matinees and some remained open until 3:30 a.m. Among the opulent landmark movie houses in New York were the Paramount, Radio City Music Hall, State, Strand, Capitol, and Roxy, shown here in an undated photograph. (Courtesy of Terri Stevens Norbeck.)

Desi Arnaz and his rumba band, and his wife actress Lucille Ball, who was informally hostessing, were big box-office draws for the May 1946 Jane Froman show. Desi Arnaz was held over and continued to pull in a major part of the proceeds for the next show, starring Peter Lind Hayes, shown here in a 1949 photograph. Peter Lind Hayes, a talented new comedian and master of mimicry, became a popular Copa performer, along with his wife Mary Healy. Additional support for the show was provided by Raul and Eva Reyes, Julie Wilson, Bob Johnston, Lynn Barrett, Joey Gilbert, and the Copa Girls. Simultaneously a Copacabana Revue—an abbreviated version of the club's show—with Peter Lind Hayes, Desi Arnaz, and Julie Wilson, along with Lee Sherman and Beatrice Seckler, George Prentice, and Bob Johnston and Janet Gaylord was presented at the Roxy Theatre. (Courtesy of AP Images.)

Doubling, performing five shows a day at the Roxy and three a night at the Copa, was common during the early forties. They performed the first show in the morning followed by three more shows at the Roxy, ran over for the first show at the Copa, returned to the Roxy for the last show, then back to the Copa for the midnight and 2:00 a.m. shows. At times during the Copa's history special events men were hired just to work out the logistics of doubling. The girls in this 1949 photograph were hired for the Roxy stage show only (not doubling). (Courtesy of Terri Stevens Norbeck.)

Casting calls went out for the film *Copacabana*, starring Groucho Marx and Carmen Miranda. The only girl selected at the main audition for a screen contract as a cast member was Chickie Winslow of Flatbush, Brooklyn, who is shown here in a September 30, 1946, photograph. (Courtesy of AP Images.)

One of the most memorable events of 1946 occurred in early fall when Phil Silvers was booked to appear at the Copa with Rags Ragland, who died suddenly two weeks prior to their opening. Club operatives insisted that Silvers fulfill the contract but he did not know if he could. Frank Sinatra told Silvers he could not make it because he was in the middle of filming *It Happened in Brooklyn*. After finishing a depressing dinner show, Silvers sat anxiously in his dressing room. When he looked up, he saw Frank Sinatra standing there, smiling. He had flown in to play his stooge, to fill in for Ragland. At the start of the next show Silvers asked if there was anyone famous in the audience. He gave a signal to ringside-seated Sinatra, who walked onto the floor. The crowd went wild. They clowned, included Julie Wilson in one of their bits, and Sinatra sat down. Sinatra came back to take a bow and Silvers asked him if they could take one for Ragland. Frank Sinatra walked off a hero. Silvers (right) is shown with Sinatra and Gloria De Haven in a 1944 photograph. (Courtesy of AP Images.)

Eddie Fisher was singing with Charlie Ventura's band in Larchmont, New York, when he got his big break to audition at the Copa in 1946 at the age of 17. Monte Proser hired him but told him to come back in a few months after he turned the legal age of 18. Young Eddie Fisher spent the summer at Grossinger's, singing with Eddie Ashman's band, and returned to New York in the fall for his Copa debut as production singer for the Joe E. Lewis show. He sang and danced with the beautiful Samba Sirens (including girlfriend Joan Wynn) in the lavish production numbers, warming up the audience for the stars of the show. As production singer, he performed several numbers with his female counterpart, a male dancer and his partner, and the line of girls. On one occasion, Celebrity Night, he went out onto the floor alone–and stole the show. After that, Proser asked him to stay on as production singer for the next show. Eddie Fisher is shown here in a 1953 photograph. (Courtesy of AP Images.)

The film *Copacabana* featured cameo appearances by *Variety* editor Abel Green (left), syndicated columnists Louis Sobol (center), with Joan Wynne on his lap, and Earl Wilson (right), shown in the Copa Girls' dressing room in an October 8, 1946, photograph. (Courtesy of Bettmann/Corbis.)

Fledgling performer Sid Caesar made his nightclub debut at the Copa on New Year's Day 1947. He met with instant success and his career took off after his Copa run. New in this winter edition was Michael Durso's orchestra, which would become a mainstay of the Copa shows over the years. Also notable was Hilliard and Mysel's "One Brazilian in a Million" that followed the coffee song onto the charts.

Carmen Miranda's April 1947 booking as Copacabana headliner was part of a new publicity strategy for her, serving as a live trailer, to promote one of her films. *Copacabana* was scheduled to premiere in New York in July 1947. She had traveled to New York with her husband David Sebastian, who was an assistant to Sam Coslow, coproducer with Monte Proser of *Copacabana*. The layout of her Copa show was worked around the movie's theme, with Carmen Miranda singing five songs from *Copacabana*, including "Let's Do the Copacabana" as her finale. In the movie, Groucho Marx played an unscrupulous theatrical agent, Lionel Q. Devereaux, whose only client, explosive Brazilian entertainer Carmen Novarro posed as both a French chanteuse and fireball Bahiana to fool the ersatz Copacabana nightclub owner into signing her for two different singing jobs. Other cast members included Copa performers Raul and Eva Reyes, dancer Dee Turnell, and Copa Girls Toni Kelly and Jill Meredith. The *Copacabana* movie poster, shown here, was designed by Latino illustrator Mora.

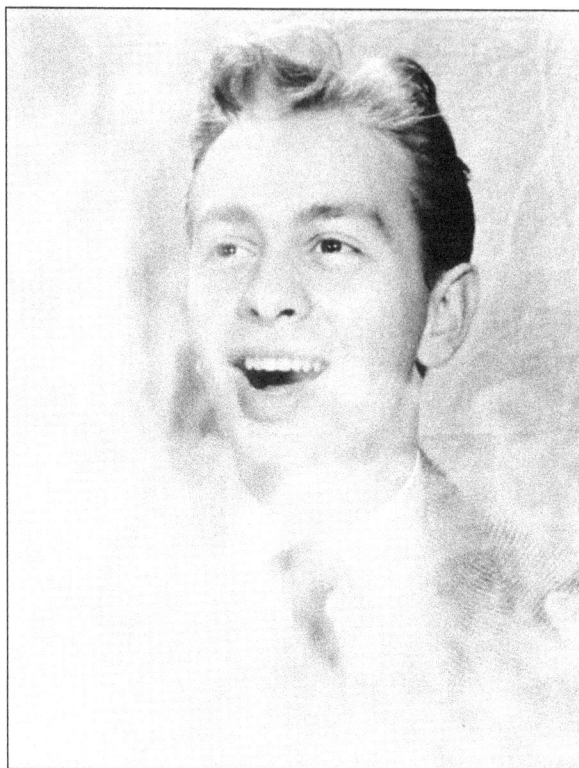

On the bill for the May 1947 prom season show, with headliner Mitzi Green, was the youngest talent ever to perform to date at the Copa with top billing, Mel Tormé. This show was also noteworthy for the introduction of Bob Hilliard and Sammy Mysel's "Red Silk Stockings and Green Perfume," another chart buster. (Photograph by William P. Gottlieb; courtesy of Jazz Photos.)

Copa regulars hated Mel Tormé's performance, but the youngsters, fired up by radio disk jockeys hype, loved every minute of it. The hundreds of teenagers that were drawn and packed into the Copa by Mel Tormé typified the huge turnouts every prom season. (Courtesy of Leo Leeds.)

In April 1947, radio personality Jack Eigen began his celebrity interview program, first on WHN then on WINS. Broadcast from the lounge of the Copacabana, it brought the thrill and excitement of this world-famous nightclub into the homes of American families everywhere. The 1:00 a.m. to 4:00 a.m. nightly show was advertised with, "And in the Copa Bar . . . Jack Eigen presents the most-listened-to All Night Broadcast with a parade of Stars of Stage, Screen and Radio." The live-broadcast concept was akin to the remote hook up of the 1920s and 1930s, when a wire was laid from radio station to out-of-studio engagements. Then, as with the on-the-air talk show simultaneously broadcast from the Copa, the radio audience got an audio sensation and vicarious enjoyment of the better life. The Copa lounge became the number one watering hole for everyday New Yorkers as well as celebrities. Eigen is shown chatting with a couple of his stars, Joe E. Lewis (center) and Milton Berle (right) during his program at the Copa in an October 15, 1947, photograph. (Courtesy of Bettmann/Corbis.)

A Roberta Sherwood show four-way foldout promotional flyer designed for mailing, shown here, advertised the famous catchphrase that Jack Eigen used to titillate radio listeners. The show-business personality interview program was another successful Copa innovation. (Courtesy of Copacabana/John Juliano.)

We're At The Copa!

Where Are You?

MAIL THIS TO A FRIEND: Somebody will envy the evening of fun you're having at The Copa. If you'd like to let them know you're here, *address this folder, and give it to your waiter. We'll stamp it and mail it.*

THE COPACABANA
10 E. 60TH ST., NEW YORK, 22

the *LATER* the *GREATER*
now there's *A LATE SHOW*
in the *COPA LOUNGE*

All through the night you'll delight in the fabulous food and drink, the bright words and music, served up in the town's favorite meetin' house, the Copa Lounge. But along about ten-ish, the place really starts jumping as the famous stay-outs drop in with their pin-ups. The fun starts with a great show, featuring many of the stars from the Copa's current production, but with so much talent in the audience, it usually winds up as a wonderful surprise party. And you're invited!

NEVER A COVER OR MINIMUM

In addition to a regularly scheduled interview, Jack Eigen's show was filled with spontaneous chats with every celebrity who walked into the lounge. The glamour, up-to-the-minute delight, and the Copa magic of anything goes swept across the nation's airwaves nightly during Eigen's "Meet Me at the Copa" sessions. (Courtesy of Copacabana/John Juliano.)

Lena Horne got her first job at the Copa as a lounge act in 1945 at a time when no blacks were admitted or booked for the main room downstairs. She was instrumental in helping to break down racial barriers by making certain that her future contracts with the Copa included a clause barring any discrimination. In later years, when she went on to become a popular headliner, anyone who wanted a table got one. Lena Horne is shown in a June 1950 photograph. (Courtesy of AP Images.)

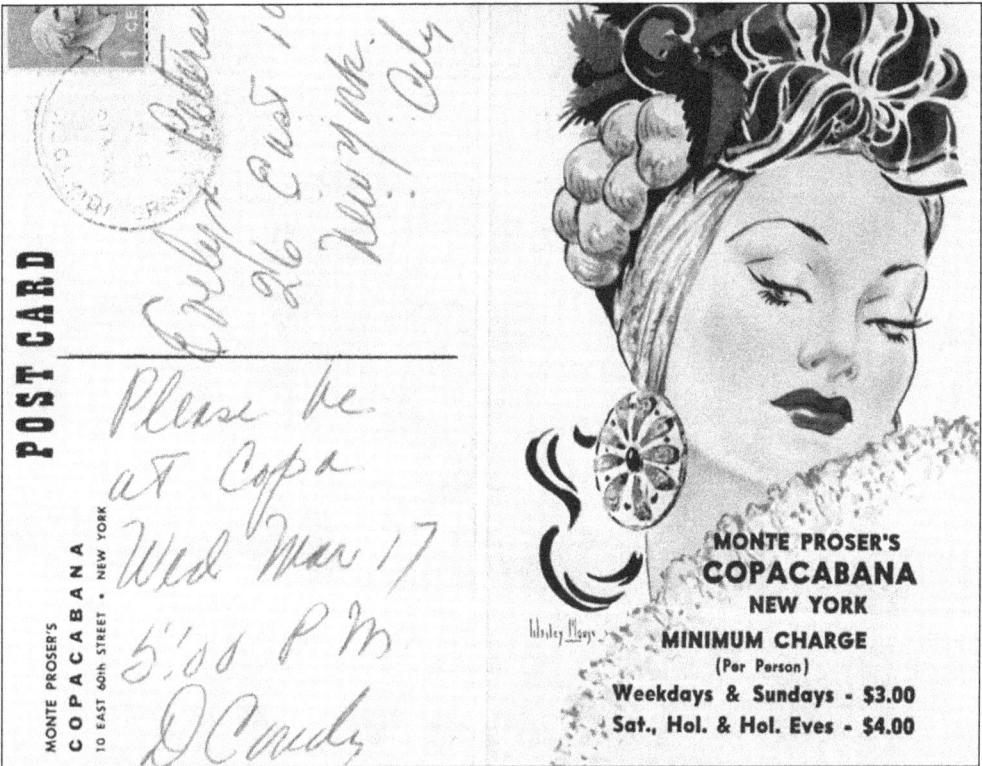

New York's modeling agencies were always a source of potential Copa Girls. Evelyn Peterson, a photographer's model, auditioned for a position in the line and was notified by postcard, shown here, that she had landed the job. (Evelyn Peterson Ohlrich.)

79

Newcomers Dean Martin and Jerry Lewis turned out to be the real stars of the Copa's April show when their act overpowered the headliner, nasal-voiced songstress-comedienne Vivian Blaine (probably best remembered for singing "A Person Could Develop a Cold" in Broadway's *Guys and Dolls* several years later), shown in an undated photograph. (© Turner Entertainment Company. A Warner Bros. Entertainment Company. All rights reserved.)

Throngs of inquisitive customers mobbed 10 East 60th Street to see the upstarts who were the new talk of the town being touted as the season's next big phenomenon, the roughhouse, hilarious team of Dean Martin and Jerry Lewis. Martin and Lewis burst into comedy stardom and had a landslide box office hit with their historic, first appearance at New York's Copacabana. The duo is shown in a 1953 photograph. (Courtesy of AP Images.)

Life magazine sent reporters and photographers over to the Copa to do a story about Dean Martin and Jerry Lewis but instead featured Evelyn Peterson in its November 1948 issue. The Texas-born hoofer, who was plugged by columnist Lee Mortimer as "the most exciting new face on Broadway," is shown with Rosalie Coleman (right) in the Copa Girls' dressing room in a 1948 photograph. (Courtesy of Evelyn Peterson Ohlrich.)

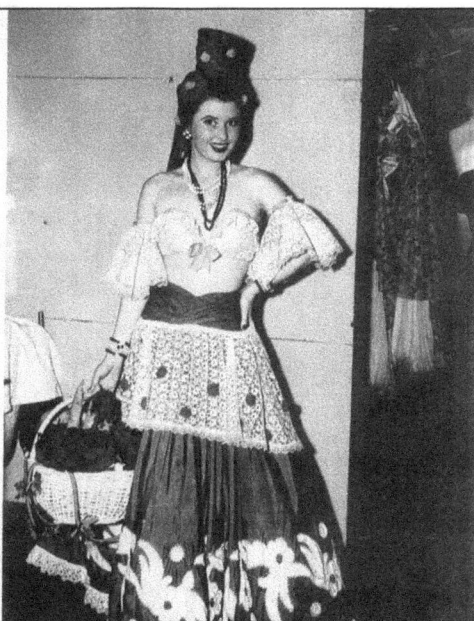

During a performance one night, Evelyn Peterson slipped, fell, and broke the zipper on her skirt. She managed to get back in the line, hang on to the basket she was holding with one hand and keep her skirt closed with the other, finish the production number, and exit the floor. She is shown wearing two Billy Livingston costumes from the Martin and Lewis show. (Courtesy of Evelyn Peterson Ohlrich.)

Only some performers felt that it was a loss of prestige to play the Copa in the slower summer months. Most comedians felt that it was the pinnacle of success to play the Paramount and the Copacabana anytime. For bright, breezy comic Joey Adams, who headlined in July 1948, it was an opportunity to break in a new act. Newlyweds Joey and Cindy Adams are shown in a 1952 photograph. (Courtesy of AP Images.)

Popular Irish tenor Morton Downy, shown here, came in as the August 1948 Copa headliner for his first New York nightclub engagement in many years. Also significant was a new tune written for the show, "May I Hold You When the Dance is Over," introduced by production singers Betty Bonney and Ralph Young (later of Sandler and Young), which hit the charts and brought more accolades for Monte Proser's Copacabana. (Courtesy of AP Images.)

Terri Stevens made her first appearance as a Copa production singer in the Joe E. Lewis 1948 fall show touted as "top-notch as its star." The young vocalist (who introduced "Unsuspecting Heart" several years later) partnered with Sonny Calello in the mostly holdover, but refurbished, song-and-dance numbers. Stevens is shown in the Copa's backstage hallway to the dressing rooms and kitchen in an undated photograph. (Courtesy of Terri Stevens Norbeck.)

Joe E. Lewis broke all records during his six weeks at the Copa, pulling in $328,000. He is shown as the center of attention in a mock New Year's Eve celebration in the Copa Girls' dressing room with, from left to right, Wendy Bartlett, Rosalie Coleman, and Frances Keegan, in a December 31, 1948, photograph. (Courtesy of AP Images.)

Dinner & Entertainment

Sponsored by

Frank Costello, Vice-Chairman of

Men's Division, Salvation Army Campaign

Monday, January 24th, 1949 at 6:30 p. m.

at the Copacabana

10 East 60th Street, New York

Entire proceeds for

Salvation Army Association

$100 per person   Dress Inf

The January 24, 1949, Salvation Army annual charity banquet, held at the Copacabana at Frank Costello's request, evolved as the scandal of the year in New York. In 1943, a wiretap on Costello's phone by New York District Attorney Frank Hogan brought national attention to a conversation between the undisputed prime minister of the underworld and newly-nominated New York supreme court judge Thomas A. Aurelio, who thanked him for his nomination and professed his undying loyalty. In 1949, Aurelio returned the favor and showed up for the $100-a-plate Salvation Army dinner, along with Costello's other friends in congress, on judge's benches, and in city hall. The press also showed up and photographed politicians and other luminaries in the company of wiseguys as they left the Copacabana, revealing Frank Costello (upon whom the author Mario Puzo based his now-famous character Don Corleone in the *Godfather*) as the skilled manipulator of the political power base in New York City in the 1940s. (Courtesy of the NY Daily News.)

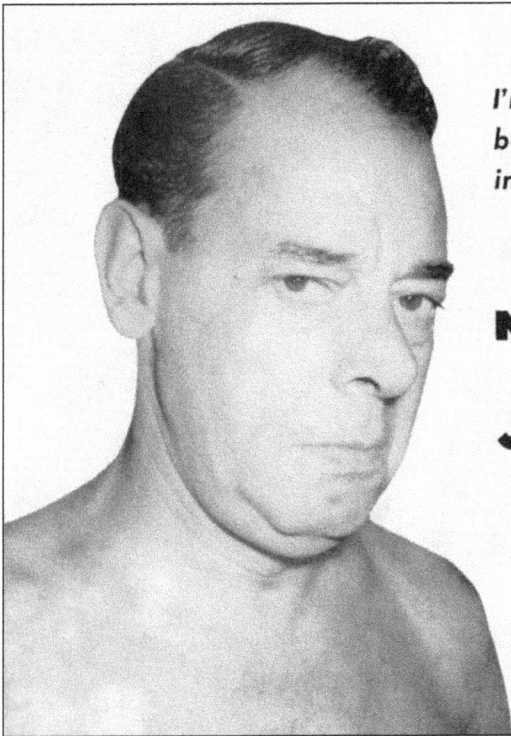

I'm still in Saratoga...
but I'll have my shirt back
in time to be here

SEPT. 8th
for The Copa's
NEW FALL REVUE

starring, in case you didn't guess,

JOE E. LEWIS
(AUSTIN MACK at the piano)

KAY STARR

CABOT & DRESDEN

JAMES BARRIE • TERRI STEVENS

and some ravishingly lovely

NEW COPA GIRLS

The Joe E. Lewis fall 1949 opening was a customarily much anticipated, satisfying event. (Courtesy of Terri Stevens Norbeck.)

The Joe E. Lewis annual fall Copa visitation was enhanced in December 1949 with the addition to the billing of Vic Damone, whose recording of "Again" was a cash box top single of that year. The 21-year-old crooner displayed remarkable poise and assurance and held the room solidly with his rich baritone delivery of traditional ballads and pop songs. He is shown here in a 1947 photograph. (Courtesy of AP Images.)

Throughout the club's history, no expense was spared in the creation of the Copa Girls' magnificent clothes that were designed and executed by the biggest names in the theatrical and fashion industries. At no time was this better exemplified than with the maroon taffeta skirt ensembles and mink accessories fashioned by one of New York's most expensive, inspired designers of the 1940s, Billy Livingston, assisted by Doug Coudy and executed by Mme Berthe. Renowned for his highly imaginative use of exquisite materials, satins, chiffons, furs, ostrich and exotic bird feathers, Livingston was highly successful as a costume designer for Broadway, nightclubs, and films, and highly sought as a couturier by celebrities and fashionable women. Posing backstage in Livingston-designed outfits from the Joe E. Lewis show are, from left to right, production singer Terri Stevens, and Copa Girls Diane Milne and Bettina Edwards, in a 1949 photograph. (Courtesy of Terri Stevens Norbeck.)

By January 1950, controlling Mafia interests were forcing Monte Proser to ease out of the Copacabana operation. It was reported that he had been spending less and less time at the Copa in recent years and engaging in musical productions and other endeavors. Although he was listed in the corporate setup as president, continued to receive his regular salary, and owned 35 percent of the club, his name was removed from the Copacabana advertisements, house literature, and awning, as shown here in an undated photograph. The Copa's general manager, Jack Entratter, who would soon be offered an attractive deal at the up-and-coming mob outpost in Las Vegas, the Sands Hotel, controlled 55 percent of the stock. Jules Podell held only 10 percent. Within a few years the nationally-televised Kefauver crime hearings would attempt to establish nightclub ownership by criminal elements. While Frank Costello would become a household name, his direct ownership of the Copacabana would never be proven. (Courtesy of Frank Driggs.)

One of the owners of the Copacabana since its inception in 1940, Jules Podell (center) had a reputation as far-reaching as that of his world-famous club at 10 East 60th Street. His often imitated "deze-dem-and-doze," gruff voice, his hard-driving, strict methodology, his often uncouth behavior, and his alleged ties with the underworld were offset by his acts of friendship, generosity, and charity, making him one of the most colorful, yet feared, but respected, men in the nightclub world. In a career that stretched back to working as a butcher and in Prohibition clubs, including a few scrapes with the law, brief jail time, small fines, and a gunshot wound to the leg, he established a reputation as the no-nonsense operator of the Kit Kat Club and then as the boss man of the Copacabana. Podell's unwavering demand for professionalism and perfection in every aspect of the club's operation was one of the key ingredients in the Copa's success. (Courtesy of Bettmann/Corbis.)

Jules "Julie" Podell was famous for sharply rapping his enormous pinky ring on the table when he wanted service or attention. With that, every head in the place would turn and every bouncer would come running. Everyone called him "Boss," and the club became known as Jules Podell's Copacabana, as shown in an undated four-way foldout advertising flyer. (Courtesy of Copacabana/John Juliano.)

Podell typically spent 12 to 16 hours a day, seven days a week at the Copa, and took only one day off a year, Yom Kippur. Unlike most nightclub operators he ran the whole business himself, hired the acts, and enforced strict policies for the Copa Girls, such as minimum age requirements, no phone calls, no notes from or mingling with customers, and a separate club entrance. He demanded proper dress code for customers and made sure everything was in perfect working order, down to the last light bulb. (Courtesy of Copacabana/John Juliano.)

Sitting at his customary table No. 1Albert (known as 1A) in the main room, Jules Podell (right) scrutinized every act, frowning if he was displeased and making the performer wonder if a contract would be renewed. He was also known to hold performers under contract at low salaries even after they became famous and commanded more monies. He is shown with Jimmy Durante and his new bride, Margie Little, in a December 1960 photograph. (Photograph by New York Journal-American; courtesy of the Harry Ransom Humanities Research Center, the University of Texas at Austin.)

Podell kept a watchful eye on the proceedings in the Copa lounge as well as the (downstairs) main room. He is shown sitting with radio talk-show host Jack Eigen in the Copa lounge discussing the Copa's drive to sell tickets for an upcoming National Sandlot baseball championship game at the Polo Grounds in an August 13, 1949, photograph. (Photograph by New York Journal-American; courtesy of the Harry Ransom Humanities Research Center, the University of Texas at Austin.)

Plaza 8-1060

Jules Podell's
copacabana
10 East 60th Street · New York

From the outset of the club's existence it was debated whether the Copa was a restaurant with entertainment or a nightclub that incidentally had good food. Jules Podell insisted it was the former. He personally oversaw the kitchen, food preparation, service, and menu (shown here) selections—involving himself in every detail—and demanded a high standard of excellence. A Copacabana program proclaimed: "The Cuisine and Kitchens are personally supervised by Jules Podell." The Copa ruler was very fastidious about the food and watched everything that went in and out of the kitchen as did his brother-in-law Sidney Robinson, who was there during the day. Podell allegedly was known to reprimand waiters who made mistakes by rapping them on the head with his ring or slapping them on the face. (Courtesy of Copacabana/John Juliano.)

hors d'oeuvres

Sea Food Copacabana 2.95

Genoa Salami 2.35
Supreme of Fruit Florida 1.25
Cherrystones 1.15
Lobster Cocktail 2.75
Crab Meat Cocktail 2.30
Jumbo Shrimp Cocktail 1.85
Assorted Juices .90
Assorted Canapes 2.50 p.p.
Filet of Herring with Sour Cream (Home Made) 1.25
*Half Seedless Grapefruit 1.10
Imp. Sardines 1.95
Hors d'Oeuvres Varies 2.95
*Bluepoints 1.25
Smoked Nova Scotia Salmon 2.50
Canape of Anchovies 1.75
Celery and Olives 1.00
Stuffed Celery 1.95
Chopped Chicken Livers, Copa 1.75
*Chilled Melon 1.20
Jumbo Shrimps, Marinara 2.75

*Available in season.

potages

Soup Du Jour .95

Cold Vichyssoise 1.10
Chicken Okra Creole 1.10
Cream of Green Peas aux Croutons .95
Petite Marmite 2.25
Green Turtle Amontillado 1.95
Cold Jellied Madrilene .95
Cream of Tomato .95
Clam Broth or Bellevue 1.10
Chicken Broth with Rice .95
Onion Soup au Gratin 1.10
Consomme Nature .95

entrees

BREAST OF CAPON, COPACABANA 5.50

Chicken Cacciatore 4.75
Chicken a la King on Toast 4.75
Tenderloin of Prime Beef, Stroganoff on Toast 6.50
Curry of Chicken, a l'Indienne with Rice 4.75
Fresh Vegetable Dinner 3.75
Half Boneless Chicken, Parmigiana 5.50
Chicken Livers Saute, on Toast 5.00
Scalopini of Veal au Marsala 5.25
Breaded Veal Cutlet, Tomato Sauce 5.25
Veal Parmigiana 5.75
Spaghetti, Chicken Livers, Caruso 3.75
Supreme of Chicken Under Bell 5.50
Arroz Con Pollo 5.50
Ravioli au Gratin 3.25
Chicken Hash, Princesse on Toast 4.75
Emince of Chicken Mexicaine with Rice 4.75

pommes de terre

Cottage Fried 1.10
Hashed in Cream 1.00
Julienne .90
Lyonnaise 1.00
French Fried .90
Candied Yams .90
Hashed Brown .90
Baked Idaho 1.00
Whipped .90
Au Gratin 1.10
Allumette .90
O'Brien 1.10
Restuffed Baked Potato 1.35

legumes

Corn Saute, Mexicaine .90
Onion Saute .80
Carrots .80
String Beans .80
Spinach (Plain) .80
New Peas .80
Succotash .90
Lima Beans .80
(Creamed) .90
Grilled Tomatoes 1.00
Stewed Fresh Tomatoes 1.25
Buttered Beets .80 Broiled Egg Plant 1.10
Braised Hearts of Celery 1.50
Broiled Mushrooms on Toast 1.95
Asparagus-Tips, Broccoli or Cauliflower 1.60
with Hollandaise or Butter Sauce

eggs

Omelette Copacabana 3.50

Scrambled Eggs 2.30
Midnight Omelette 3.50
Ham Omelette 3.10
Shirred Eggs, Opera 3.10
with Bacon, Ham or Sausages 3.10
Spanish Omelette 2.75
Poached Eggs on Toast 2.30
Omelette Nature 2.30
Eggs Benedict 3.50

rotis et grillades

Calf's Liver with Bacon 5.95
Calf Sweetbreads, Virginienne 6.25
(2) Lamb Chops 5.25
Prime Sirloin Steak 7.25
Tips of Tenderloin of Beef En Brochette 6.50
Rack of Lamb Persillade (for 2) 10.75
Mixed Grill a l'Anglaise 5.25
Long Island Duckling, Apple Sauce 5.50
Chateaubriand (for 2) 15.00
Baby Lamb Steak, Mint Jelly 5.10
Minute Steak, O'Brien Potatoes 6.00
Prime Filet Mignon 7.00
Half Spring Chicken 4.75
Bouquetiere 1.50 p.p.
Ham Steak Hawaiienne 5.10
Chopped Sirloin of Prime Beef 4.50
Chicken Livers En Brochette 5.00
Whole Boneless Broiled Chicken A La Podeh 8.50
Shashlik, Caucasian .75 (per person)
BEARNAISE OR CHORON SAUCE .75
SAUCE ROBERT .50

rarebits

Welsh Rarebit 2.40
Long Island 2.65
Golden Buck 2.90
Yorkshire Buck 3.25

We are compelled by law to collect 10% federal tax and 5% city tax

poissons

Brochette of Scallops 3.95
Crab Meat au Gratin on Toast 4.80
Lobster a la Newburg on Toast 5.25
Curried Shrimp Madras with Rice 4.95
Sea Food a l'Americaine with Rice 5.75
Frog's Legs Provencale 5.50
Lobster Americaine with Rice 6.95
South African Lobster-Tails 5.25
Seafood, Newburg on Toast 5.10
Jumbo Shrimp Creole with Rice 4.95
Curry of Seafood with Rice 5.10
Crab Meat Dewey on Toast 4.80
Lobster Thermidor or Cardinal 5.50
Scallops, Poulette on Toast 3.95
Oysters Casino 2.95
Filet of Sole, Breteuil 3.95
Whole Broiled Maine Lobster with Julienne Potatoes 5.75

Bread and Butter .50 p. p.

Stuffed Tom
Hal
Steak Tartar
SPECIAL
Half Roast
Beef Tongue

desser

Pear Helene 1.50
Parfait Copacabana
Peach Melba 1.5
Coupe aux Marrons
Crepes Suzette 3.50 Petit
Cherries Jubilee 2.75 Fruit
Baked Alaska Flambee (for
Lemon or Raspberry Sher
Chocolate, Vanilla or Strawberry
Ice-Cream Cake .80
Apple or Blueberry P

coffee, tea

Pot of Coffee or Tea with
Sanka .60
Demi-Tasse .60 Iced Tea
Postum .60
Cafe Espresso

Barbecued Spa
Egg Roll 1.50

Gai Choy Gong
Won Ton Soup

White Meat Chi
White Meat Sub
Lobster Chop Su
Chicken Chop Su
Shrimp Chow M
Lobster Chow Me
Crab Meat Chow
Butterfly Fried
Steak Kew 8.2

Chicken Foo You
Shrimp Foo You

Plain Fried Rice

Chinese Fortune

et froid

Stuffed Tomato, New Orleans 5.25
Salad, Hard Boiled Egg, Tomato 5.75
Smoked Nova Scotia Salmon 3.95
STRING BEANS, TOMATO AND POTATO SALAD
ssorted Cold Cuts 4.95   Sliced Ham 4.95
of Beef 6.95   Sliced Breast of Chicken 5.75

cheese

(Served with Toasted Crackers)

Petit Gruyere .95
Camembert .95
Roquefort 1.25   American 1.00
Swiss 1.10   Port du Salut 1.10
Cream Cheese 1.00
Bel Paese 1.00

salads

Crab Meat 4.95
Shrimp 4.75
Tomato and Lettuce 1.25
Chef's 3.95
Fruit Salad—French Dressing 3.50
Sliced Tomatoes .95
Potato Salad 1.00
Vegetable 2.50
Lobster 5.25
Caesar Salad 1.50
Tuna Fish 3.75
Cole Slaw 1.00
Salad Dressing .50 additional
Lettuce, Romaine, Chicory or Escarole 1.25
Asparagus Tips 1.95
Chiffonade 1.25
Chicken 4.50 (white meat) 1.10
Mixed Green 1.10
Hearts of Lettuce 5.75
Watercress 1.10 1.10

sandwiches

Copacabana 2.95

Steak 5.00   Club 2.95   Genoa Salami 1.95
Chicken 2.50   Western 2.40   Hot Chicken 2.85
American Cheese 1.60   Swiss Cheese 1.75   Ham and Cheese 2.20
York Ham 1.95   Chopped Chicken Liver 1.75   Beef Tongue 2.20
Imported Sardine 1.75   Tuna Fish 1.75   Melted Cheese with Bacon 1.95
Chopped Sirloin of Prime Beef with Spanish Onion 3.25   Ham and Egg 2.40
Prime Ribs of Beef 4.75 (Hot) 5.25   Smoked Nova Scotia Salmon 2.50
Sandwich Dressing .25 additional

hinese dishes

Roast Pork 2.40

SOUPS

Mein Gong with Roast Pork 1.50   Yoko Min with Egg and Roast Pork 1.75
Gai Fan Gong .85   Dun Fa Gong 1.10   Gai Mein Gong (chicken noodle) .85

ENTREES

Mushrooms, Water Chestnuts and Bamboo Shoots 4.25   Crab Meat Chop Suey with Mushrooms 4.10
with Almonds 4.25   Moo Goo Gai Pan 4.50   Dark Meat Chicken Chow Mein 3.60
d Bamboo Shoots 4.50   Subgum Chicken Chow Mein (white meat only) with Almonds 4.25
0   Roast Pork Chow Mein with Mushrooms 3.95   Chinese Cabbage with Roast Pork 3.95
.10   Chicken Lo Mein 4.50   Green Pepper Steak with Mushrooms and Fresh Tomatoes 4.25
Bamboo Shoots 4.50   Beef, Oyster Sauce 4.75   Lobster Cantonese 4.95
Sweet & Sour Pork with Pineapple, Green Peppers, Fresh Tomatoes and Chinese Pickles 4.50
Beef Chop Suey 4.25   Beef Chow Mein 4.25
Lobster Soong 5.75   Shrimps Cantonese 4.50

OMELETTES

ts, Mushroom Sauce 2.50   Crab Meat Foo Young, Water Chestnuts, Mushroom Sauce 3.20
ushroom Sauce 2.95   Roast Pork Foo Young, Water Chestnuts, Mushroom Sauce 2.75
obster Foo Young, Water Chestnuts, Mushroom Sauce 3.50

FRIED RICE

d Rice 1.00   Pork Fried Rice 1.00   Shrimp Fried Rice 1.25   Lobster Fried Rice 1.25

DESSERTS

Kumquat 1.10   Chinese Mixed Fruit 1.10   Almond Cookies .90
Pot of Chinese Tea .60

The club's literature proudly stated: "CUISINE A LA COPA. Just marvelous! This is because the Copa has a reputation to live up to . . . a reputation for the finest in everything. Master chefs whip up outstanding gourmet menus in kitchens any woman would adore. Service is a happy, courteous experience. Surprisingly enough, Copa Cuisine will cost you far less than most of our town's finest restaurants." A Copa program from the 1950s advertised: "THE CHINESE CUISINE. The Copa is famous for is oriental dishes, and there's a reason why. We maintain a separate Chinese unit in our kitchen, staffed by the finest native chefs. If you are a lover of Chinese food you will agree with those who have said that, there is no better Chinese food served anywhere. (Courtesy of Copacabana/John Juliano.)

The chart-topping success of Frankie Laine's 1950 recording of "Mule Train" prompted Frank Sinatra to do an impersonation of his rival male vocalist during one of his Copa performances, shown here in an undated photograph. (Courtesy of Motion Picture and Television Photo Archive.)

Skitch Henderson, shown here in a 1950 photograph, was musical director for Frank Sinatra's Lucky Strike-sponsored radio show and his accompanist and conductor for his March 1950 Copa opening. The frenzied pace, along with the emotional and professional pressures in Frank Sinatra's life, took its toll, and one night, while singing "Bali Ha'i," he lost his voice due to a submucosal hemorrhage and was forced to cancel his engagement. (Courtesy of AP Images.)

Singer Toni Arden made her Copa debut in the May 1950 Dean Martin and Jerry Lewis show and drew wide acclaim for her showmanship, diverse pacing and material, and exciting arrangements. She is shown seated (second from left) with some of her fans and friends between shows in April 1951. Seated to her right is former Copa Girl Donna Lee Hickey, who would soon adopt the stage name May Wynn and become known for her role in *The Caine Mutiny*. (Courtesy of Toni Arden.)

Comedian Henny Youngman came into the Copa and brought 1950 to a close with his trademark one-liners, like his famous "Take my wife, please!" and rapid-fire delivery of gags. He is shown making preparations for New Year's Eve in a December 29, 1950, photograph with Copa Girls, from left to right (first row) Pat Wray and Pat Hardy; (second row) Judy Tyler and Chris Hart. (Courtesy of AP Images.)

By March 1951, Billy Eckstine's name was bringing both marquee and entertainment clout to the Copa billing. The robust baritone who had a big hit with "Jealousy," considered his Copa booking a personal triumph after having worked his way up from 52nd Street swing spots to a newly-signed 10-year recording contract and movie deal with MGM. (Photograph by Al Stewart from *View From the Bandstand*.)

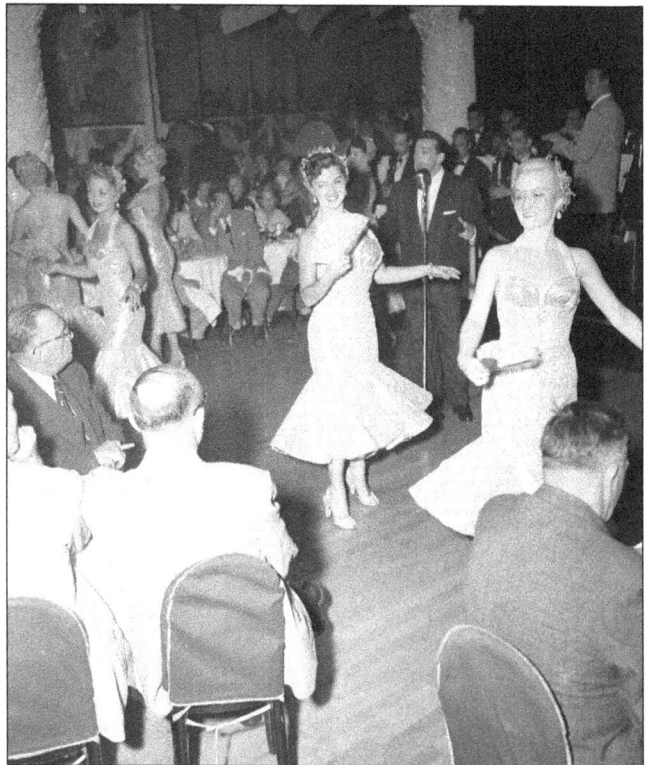

Former model and beauty contest winner Pat Hardy, who later became well known to television viewers, is shown center stage as a Copa Girl in a September 5, 1951, photograph taken during one of the production numbers. (Courtesy of AP Images.)

A perennial crowd-pleaser at the Copa, the big-hearted Schnoz, Jimmy Durante, is shown practicing a bebop number with them on March 27, 1952, in preparation for an 11-night stand at the Copa. (Courtesy of AP Images.)

By 1952, the Copa lost several headliners, including Tony Martin, Lena Horne, and Frank Sinatra, who switched to Bill Miller's (formerly Ben Marden's) Riviera in Fort Lee, New Jersey. The change in venue seemed to stem from the fact that, although salaries were comparable, the Copa's three-shows-nightly policy was less appealing to performers than the Riviera's two shows and no discrimination policy. (Courtesy of Dexter Press.)

Johnnie Ray was an even bigger sensation than Frank Sinatra—but moved the audience to the same degree of woe and ecstasy—when he headlined the Copa for the first time in April 1952. His huge success as well as his writhing, tormented performance, going down on the floor and strangling words with a tortured, crying voice was unlike anything that had ever been seen at the Copa. (Courtesy of Bettmann/Corbis.)

Johnnie Ray's first show was a flop because he was an unknown and there had been no publicity, but for some reason, his second show was overbooked. In the audience on his opening night was Marlene Dietrich, Yul Brenner, Nat Cole, and others, all within shouting distance, as well as his sweetheart Rosemary Clooney, shown with him in an April 30, 1952, photograph. (Photograph by New York Journal-American; courtesy of the Harry Ransom Humanities Research Center, the University of Texas at Austin.)

In 1952, Jack Entratter accepted an offer to be vice-president of the new Sands Hotel on Highway 91 in Las Vegas, representing his own as well as Frank Costello's interests. It was scheduled to open for business on December 15, 1952, with Danny Thomas already booked as the opening act. The Sands's Copa Room would shortly become the new hot spot. (Courtesy of Colourpicture Publication.)

Comedian Jack Carter, shown here, along with the New York bow of Jimmy McHugh's Song Stars of Tomorrow, followed Danny Thomas into the Copa in April 1953. The Copacabana continued to offer new, innovative, top-notch acts, such as Jimmy McHugh's troupe and opera diva Helen Traubel, who would headline later that year. (Courtesy of AP Images.)

Jimmy Durante takes a minute on June 10, 1954, to speak with air traffic controllers before boarding a plane for Boston after completing a three-week engagement at the Copacabana. He is assisted by ex-Copa Girl June Tolley, who now worked with Durante on television and traveled with the Durante troupe. Ten years had passed since the sensational "Columbus Day Riot at the Paramount," when Frank Sinatra made teenage girls scream, swoon, and faint. Now America was about to witness the emergence of another entertainer, Elvis Presley, whose music as well as erotic gyrations would create mass hysteria among a new generation of adolescent females. Ten years later it would happen again with the Beatles. (Courtesy of AP Images.)

Five

THE WINDS OF CHANGE
1954–1963

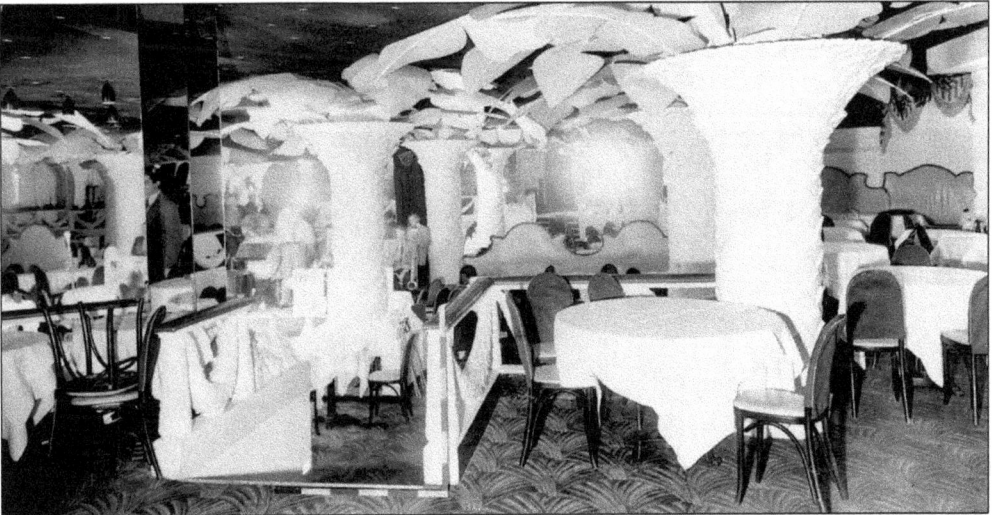

While the onset of Elvis Presley's prestardom period had no immediate impact on the Copacabana, his rise to fame was a sign of changing times. He was the first and greatest rock and roll success, and he initiated a craze that dominated the field of popular music in the 1950s. Rock and roll was everywhere, including the Copa. It was a time of simple pleasures, peace, unprecedented prosperity, migration to suburbia, and the advent of the commercial jet airplane. Americans were mesmerized by television. Its tremendous growth during the 1950s altered forever the shape of popular culture. The burgeoning passion for this new form of entertainment put theater, movies, and nightclubs on the defensive as they, in turn, had done to vaudeville. No longer was it necessary for families to travel from suburbs to cities to be entertained. On the other hand, television made many new stars and expanded the careers of established ones, including a number who regularly headlined the Copa. In the mid-1950s, four large columns in the main room of the Copacabana were removed. Visibility was greatly improved, and Copa operatives were pleased with the clear floor span. (Courtesy of Frank Driggs.)

In early April 1954, Sammy Davis Jr. fulfilled a life-long dream when the Will Mastin Trio, featuring Sammy Davis Jr., made their New York café debut as headliners at the Copacabana. Listening to Jack Eigen's celebrity interview program, and sometimes watching from the doorway of a building across the street, he wondered if he would ever play the Copa. (Photograph by Milton H. Greene; courtesy of the Archives/Joshua Greene.)

They danced as a unit when Sammy Davis Jr. came on, then he took over while his father and uncle stood at the sidelines. The audience seemed to know their story, that, as the young showman had honed his talents and had gained solo prominence, the act became his showcase, with the two older men providing tap and soft-shoe background. Conductor Morty Stevens (second row, center) is shown here behind Sammy Davis Jr. (Photograph by Milton H. Greene; courtesy of the Archives/Joshua Greene.)

102

The show's opening production number was backed by Mike Durso's Copacabana Orchestra and featured singer Sandy Evans, a line of eight lovely Copa Girls, bedecked in flashy Michi (executed by Mme Berthe) costumes, the dance team of Betty Lorraine and Chuck Brunner, followed by ballroomologists Page and Bray, and songstress Mary Small. (Photograph by Milton H. Greene; courtesy of the Archives/Joshua Greene.)

A series of hit records, in particular *Because of You* and *Cold, Cold Heart,* had made March 1956 Copa headliner Tony Bennett one of the most popular recording artists of the early 1950s. With a steadfast commitment to sing only great songs, he withstood pressure to get on the rock-and-roll bandwagon and held Copa audiences captive with his warm, husky delivery of pop songs, ballads, and show tunes. (Photograph by Don Hunstein for Sony Music.)

Former burlesque and vaudeville comedian, Broadway and film actor, and star of his own television show, Red Buttons, shown here in a 1948 photograph, was much sought after by nightclub operators in the mid-1950s. Jules Podell finally succeeded in luring him to headline the Copacabana in April 1956, with sub-billed Eileen Barton, best remembered for her smash hit "If I Knew You Were Coming, I'd've Baked a Cake." (Photograph by James Kollar Studios; courtesy of Culver Pictures.)

Handsome, charismatic, hit recording star Tony Martin returned to the Copa after the shuttering of Bill Miller's Riviera, where he had been playing. As always the relaxed performer with the fine voice charmed the standing-room-only audiences, which were tightly packed to increase capacity. He is shown arriving in New York from London in a September 1956 photograph. (Courtesy of AP Images.)

A Star is Born at the COPA

I GOT LOST IN HIS ARMS

LAZY RIVER

GEE BUT I HATE TO GO HOME ALONE

THE GLORY OF LOVE

JULES PODELL'S COPACABANA

MEMBER OF THE DINERS' CLUB

10 EAST 60 • PL 8-0900

A middle-aged mother and housewife, unknown and broke, Roberta Sherwood became one of the all-time great nightclub success stories. She captured the hearts of audiences everywhere with her strong, sweet voice, her simple, sincere approach to ballads, and her trademark banging of a cymbal and tapping her foot. Her opening night at the Copacabana, June 7, 1956, was hailed by one reviewer as "a triumph of the first magnitude." (Courtesy of Copacabana/John Juliano.)

The night of July 24, 1956, was an overwhelming one for the many Dean Martin and Jerry Lewis fans, friends, and curiosity-seekers that jammed the Copacabana to watch one of the greatest comedy duos of all time work together for the very last time. Martin (left) and Lewis are shown rehearsing at Manhattan's Nola Studios for a 1954 opening at the Copa. (Courtesy of AP Images.)

One of the most highly publicized disturbances at the Copa involved a fight between some customers and several of the New York Yankees, on May 16, 1957. Standing outside New York City Criminal Courts building after a grand jury returned No Bill on felonious assault charges against Hank Bauer are, from left to right, Mickey Mantle, Billy Martin, and Hank Bauer and his wife. (Courtesy of AP Images.)

When clown-at-heart Martha Raye opened at the Copacabana on October 17, 1957, she showed a different side of herself besides the singing, dancing, and comedic talent so familiar to her audiences. She hit her peak with straight singing, revealing a new artistic facet of her career. She is shown here in a September 27, 1956, photograph. (Courtesy of AP Images.)

On the bill with Martha Raye was young Steve Lawrence. He had made a name for himself on Steve Allen's old *Tonight Show*, which led to a recording contract and hit record (*Poinciana*), guest spots on some of televisions's top variety shows, and a romance with songstress Eydie Gorme. The future, frequent Copa headliners are shown in a January 1969 photograph. (Courtesy of AP Images.)

Copacabana waiter James Kouvales laughs approvingly at a joke told by Marty Allen (right, rear) and Mitch DeWood, a comedy team that rose rapidly in popularity after the breakup of Dean Martin and Jerry Lewis. Allen and DeWood are shown at the Copa in a January 28, 1958, photograph. (Courtesy of AP Images.)

Peggy Lee was the Copa's 1958 Valentine's offering in her first appearance at the club. After a rough few minutes during her opening numbers, when customers had to accustom themselves to her deliberate, whispering style, they became so captivated by her phrasing and indefinable aura that their clamoring produced three encore sets and an authentic beg-off. Crowds are shown here lining up for a Peggy Lee show at the Copacabana. (Courtesy of Peggy Lee Associates LLC.)

The late February 1958 pairing of Tony Bennett and the comedy team of Rowan and Martin was hailed as a winning bill entertainment-wise. Although Dan Rowan and Dick Martin had worked individually, it was not until they teamed up that they rose to prominence and became the sweethearts of television variety shows and nightclubs. Rowan (top) and Martin are shown in a June 8, 1957, photograph. (Courtesy of AP Images.)

The February 1958 Tony Bennett show was distinguished by a unique musical accompaniment of a complete tympani section (Latin American rhythmists, Sabu and Candido) and flutist (Herbie Mann). The Copa show was so successful that Tony Bennett took Candido on the road with him for club dates in Chicago, Brooklyn, and Montreal. (Photograph by Don Hunstein for Sony Music.)

With an enhanced rhythm backup Tony Bennett delivered an innovative and exciting performance for this Copa appearance, demonstrating how much he had grown as a performer over the past few years. (Photograph by Don Hunstein for Sony Music.)

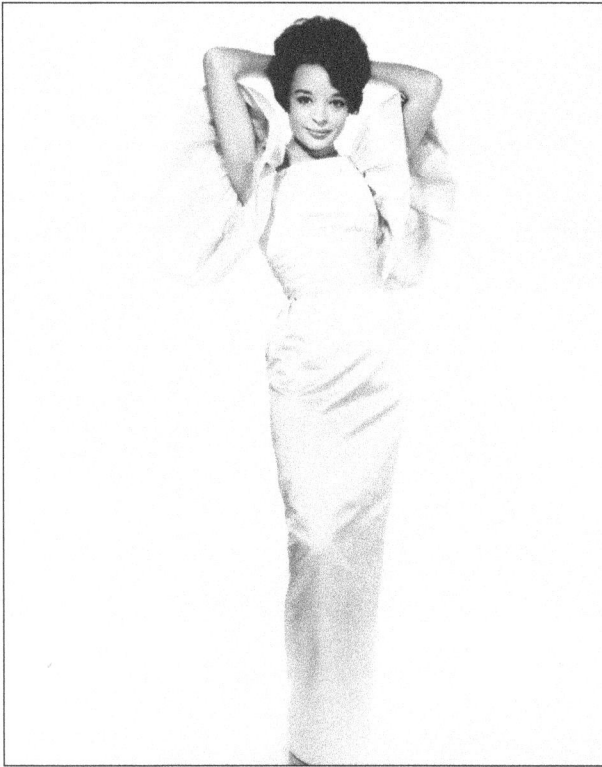

One of the youngest headliners in the history of the Copacabana was Jill Corey. The attractive performer had risen to national prominence through her appearances on the Dave Garroway, Ed Sullivan, and Johnny Carson television shows, a 1953 *Life* cover story, and her 1957 biggest hit single "Love Me to Pieces." She is shown in the pink gown that she wore for her opening night at the Copa on August 21, 1958. (Courtesy of Albert J. Kopec.)

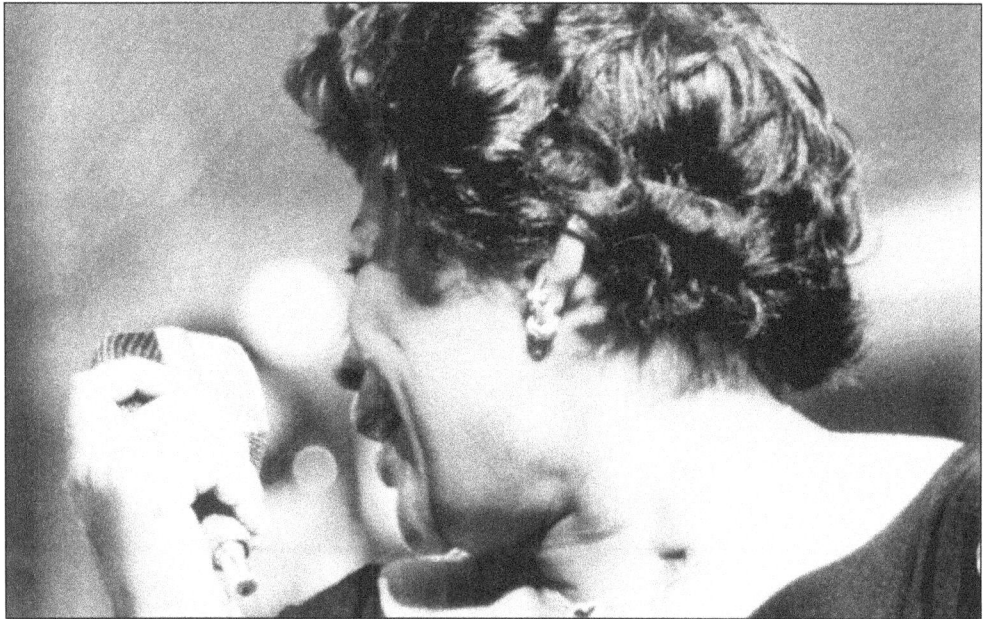

On his way back to Hollywood for daughter Nancy's high school graduation in June 1958, Frank Sinatra stopped to see Ella Fitzgerald, who was making her second appearance at the Copacabana. Weary from encores brought on by an exuberant prom crowd, she looked over to Sinatra, who strode onto the floor and joined her in a chorus of "Moonlight in Vermont," followed onstage by Vic Damone, then Johnny Mathis. (Courtesy of the Ella Fitzgerald Charitable Foundation.)

The 1959 Valentine slot was filled with a Jules Podell presentation of a rising new star, singer Johnny Mathis, who had become one of the leading Columbia Records artists in the pop single and album fields over the previous two years. He brought in a half-dozen of his own musicians to be certain of custom-made arrangements for a show that relied heavily on his best-selling hits. He is shown in a March 1958 photograph. (Courtesy of AP Images.)

The 1959 spring season at the Copa was launched with headliner Frankie Laine. While his easy floor delivery belied the effort that went into a belting delivery style, singer Laine delighted his many fans with an exuberant and exciting performance, creating a strong impact with a repertoire of his many hits. He is shown here in an undated photograph. (Courtesy of Frankie Laine.)

For the first time in many years, the Copa resumed a three-show nightly schedule that was normally reserved for the busy weekends. On Saturday, May 16, 1959, during the smash two-week stand of Louis Prima and Keely Smith, there were four shows. Billed as *The Wildest*, the run did a record-breaking take of an estimated $250,000. (Courtesy of AP Images.)

Nat King Cole did dynamite box office for the Copa when he returned as headliner in October 1959. A great natural pop singer with superb projection, showmanship, a captivating singing style, and repertoire of hits, he always held audiences mesmerized. He is shown in a November 7, 1958, photograph seated between injured Brooklyn Dodgers' catcher Roy Campanella, who was allowed to return home after nearly a year of rehabilitation following a car accident that left him paralyzed, and his wife Ruthe Campanella. (Courtesy of AP Images.)

Jack Entratter vacated his job as long-time general manager of the Copacabana in 1952 to become vice president and purchaser of entertainment at the Las Vegas Sands Hotel, and immediately used his old Copa connections to book stars for the Sands' Copa Room. Backstage at the Copa Room are, from left to right, Dean Martin, Frank Sinatra, and Jack Entratter. (Original work the Property of University of Nevada-Las Vegas, Las Vegas, Nevada.)

Huge salaries offered by new Las Vegas hot spots overpowered the Copacabana's talent budget, further contributing to its operating woes. Wayne Newton, now known as "Mr. Las Vegas," had gotten a start in the music business as a Copa lounge act.

113

In 1959, Bobby Darin emerged as one of the hottest new stars in recent years, with a Grammy Award for "Mack the Knife" and another for Best New Artist of the Year, formidable album sales, guest spots on all the top television variety shows, and cover and feature magazine stories, all setting the stage for his record-breaking June 1960 Copa engagement. (Courtesy of AP Images.)

Shown in an impromptu jam session in the Copa lounge in the early 1960s are, from left to right, Bobby Darin at the piano, unidentified, and Sammy Davis Jr. at the drums. (Courtesy of Jimmy Scalia, official Bobby Darin archivist.)

Six

AN ERA GONE BY
1964–

The 1960s was a decade of youth, hippies, and happenings. Out went pillbox hats, white gloves, and feminine garb. In now were long hair, tie-dyes, and jeans. Innocence, a notion of exclusivity, and the sacred image of the Copa Girl vanished as sexual permissiveness and explicitness became the order of the day. In spite of a changing world and a downturn in business (the Copa lost money in 1963 for the first time since it opened), the Copacabana retained its aura of fun and excitement. One of the exciting highlights of this era is the now-famous crime classic that started with a romance between Copa hat check girl, Carol Galvin, and New York Police Department detective Eddie "Popeye" Egan, and turned into a true-life odyssey known as *The French Connection*. It began at the Copa on the night of Saturday, October 7, 1961, when Egan and his partner, Sonny Grasso, left the club to tail a suspicious patron and ended, months later, with their return to the Copa to celebrate. (Courtesy of Twentieth Century-Fox.)

The Copacabana had never had more patrons or taken in as much money in its 24-year history as it did during the May 1964 run of Sammy Davis Jr. He is shown with actress Elizabeth Taylor and her husband actor Richard Burton in his Copa dressing room after his opening on April 30, 1964. (Courtesy of AP Images.)

While everyone seemed to agree that Sam Cooke had failed his first time at the Copa in March 1958, mainly because he was not fully prepared, his summer 1964 appearance was a huge success. He is shown performing during this engagement in a photograph that was used for the album cover of a live recording, *Sam Cooke at the Copa*. (Courtesy of AP Images.)

A new record for the club was set by Jerry Vale, who became the first artist to appear at the Copacabana three times within one year. It was a testament to his popularity and the durability of his long-standing association with the club's management that Jules Podell asked him to follow in the footsteps of Joe E. Lewis, who recently died, and open the Copa every fall. (Courtesy of AP Images.)

JULES PODELL ANNOUNCES

the Copa
debut
of an
exciting
new
star!

JIMMY ROSELLI

JIMMY ROSELLI
PAT COOPER

• DENNIS BELL •
The World Famous Copa Girls
JOSEPH MELE and the COPACABANA ORCHESTRA
FRANK MARTI and the COPA CHA-CHA BAND

Member of The Diners' Club

Staged by DOUGLAS COUDY
Music and Lyrics by SAMMY MYSELS & DICK SANFORD
Orchestrations by JOSEPH MELE
Costumes designed by BILLY LIVINGSTON
Executed by MME. BERTHE
Coiffures by LARRY MATHEWS

JULES PODELL'S

COPACABANA
10 E. 60th ST.   Plaza 8-0900

In one of the most heavily-attended opening nights in a long time, newcomer Jimmy Roselli and comedian Pat Cooper attracted crowds that lined up outside for blocks on February 25, 1965. It was an unbelievable night that began with Sammy Davis Jr.'s introduction of the debuting Roselli and ended up with Roselli as the new talk of the town. (Courtesy of Copacabana/John Juliano.)

117

118

Y BISHOP

SAMMY DAVIS, JR.

NAT KING COLE

JACK E. LEONARD

JIMMY ROSELLI

STEVE LAWRENCE & EYDIE GORME

JOHNNY MATHIS

LOUIS PRIMA

PETULA CLARK

JERRY VALE

The crowning achievement of a Copacabana headliner was to be awarded the Copa's symbol of success—the Copa Bonnet—the equivalent of a nightclub academy award. Over the years only the most talented performers and the biggest names in show business were honored with the Copa Bonnet. (Courtesy of Copacabana/John Juliano.)

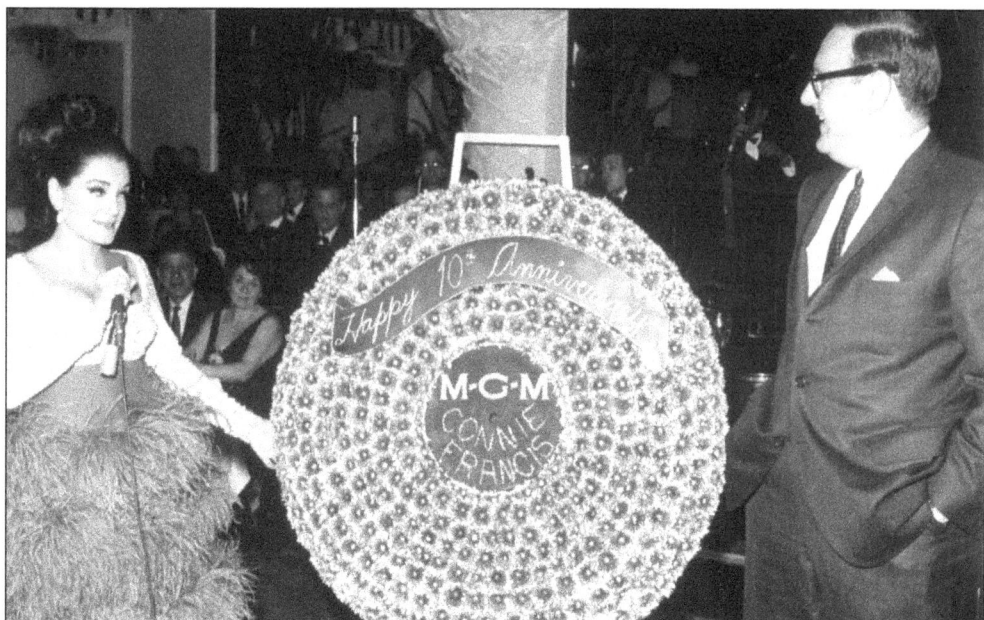

Often called America's Sweetheart of Song and one of the most successful female vocalists of all time, Connie Francis enjoyed a long, gratifying association with the Copacabana. She is shown here during her standing-room-only February 1967 appearance, on the occasion of her 10th anniversary with MGM Records, being presented with a large recording-disk-shaped floral tribute by MGM president Mort Nasitir. (Courtesy of Pat Niglio.)

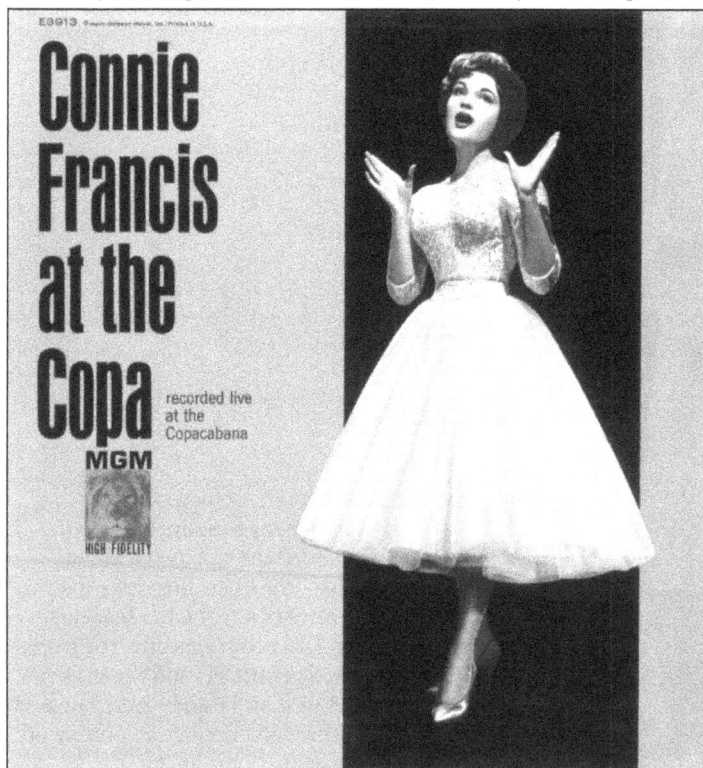

Many live recordings were made at the Copacabana throughout its history, including those by Paul Anka, Petula Clark, Sam Cooke, Bobby Darin, Jimmy Durante, Tony Martin, Edith Piaf, and Jackie Wilson. (Photograph by James Kriegsmann; courtesy of Pat Niglio.)

The mayhem produced by Tom Jones's sensational May 1969 show was reminiscent of Johnnie Ray's appearance a few years back. The British rocker, who brought to the Copa a different element of power, drive, and energy, had crowds lined up around the block. (Courtesy of AP Images.)

Chart-buster Dionne Warwick, in her very first appearance at the Copacabana in May 1968, brought an appealing freshness to the prom season. Fortified by good songs written for her by the winning pop musical team of Burt Bacharach and Hal David, she presented a swinging, lively set of hit songs and standards. She is shown in the doorway of the star's dressing room at the Copacabana in a 1969 photograph. (Photograph by Richard Henry; courtesy of Byron Motley.)

The Copacabana kicked off the 1968 fall season with headliner Jerry Vale and a lineup that included some new production songs, dancer Patti D'Beck, the Copa Girls, and Errol Dante, the last production singer in the history of the club. Dante and D'Beck are shown here surrounded by the Copa Girls in a December 1968 photograph. (Courtesy of Errol Dante.)

Errol Dante (left) was temporarily relieved of his production singing duties in late October 1968 for the standing-room-only Don Rickles show, which was sold out every night. (Courtesy of Errol Dante.)

As a result of budget cutbacks the Copa house band was cut from 10 musicians to a six-piece band, which played for between-show dancing as well as the line-of-girls-only production numbers. The band is shown here with extra musicians brought in to play for a Paul Anka show. (Courtesy of Morty Trautman.)

The 1971 fall season, which marked the 31st anniversary of the Copacabana, was ushered in by comedian Pat Henry. He was followed by WNEW-Radio disk jockey and singer, Julius La Rosa, shown here, best known for his 1953 smash hit, "Eh, Cumpari." (Photograph by Maurice Seymour; courtesy of Ron Seymour.)

The ongoing wiseguy presence at the Copacabana was underscored in the later years by an incident that began with a Copa champagne birthday celebration hosted by Mafia boss Joseph (Crazy Joe) Gallo, shown here. In the pre-dawn hours of April 7, 1972, Gallo, his wife, and friends got into their black Cadillacs and headed downtown to Umberto's Clam House, where flamboyant Gallo was gunned down in one of the more spectacular gangland slayings on record. (Courtesy of Thom Ang.)

After a 1972 summer closing accompanied by a generally uncertain future for New York nightclubs, there were rumors that the Copa might shutter again at the end of the 1973 prom season. When the club closed that June, after Tony Orlando and Dawn had made every show memorable with a spirited rendition of their hit single "Tie a Yellow Ribbon 'Round the Ole Oak Tree," everyone knew it was the end of an era. Tony Orlando is shown here in a c. 1977 photograph by Neal Preston. (Courtesy of Corbis.)

Jules Podell died in September 1973, and the Copacabana remained vacant for several years. It reopened in 1976 as a disco (downstairs) and cabaret (upstairs) and featured acts like vocalist Kathy Walsh Moran, with Mike Moran (pianist), and Herman Wright (bassist), shown in a January 1976 photograph. (Courtesy of Mike Moran.)

Eartha Kitt, who used the date primarily as a site to record an album for Casablanca, Redd Fox, and Ray Charles, shown here in a 1979 photograph, were booked for brief stints in the years that followed. (Courtesy of AP Images.)

New owners bought the rights to the Copacabana name and the club was moved in 1993 to a new, much bigger, $3 million location at West 57th Street. Terri Stevens (left), Julie Wilson (second row, left), and a group of World Famous Copacabana Girls alumni club members are shown holding up a banner at the new club. In October 2002, the Copacabana relocated again to a huge 50,000 square foot, tri-level former warehouse at West 34th Street, retaining the trademark white palm trees, Copa Girl logo, the Copa Girls, and the Cabana Boys. In recent years, alumnae of the famed Copa Girl dancing lines have been featured as guests on television and their dinner-dance reunions have attracted many celebrities in addition to raising significant funds for charitable organizations. They still have the festive beat of the old Copa days in their hearts and can still kick up their signature and trademark gorgeous legs, along with their showgirl line-up of stories about the headline acts that once graced the magical room, three steps up and one flight down, called the Copacabana. (Photograph by Frank Verna; courtesy of Terri Stevens Norbeck.)

INDEX

Visit us at
arcadiapublishing.com

www.ingramcontent.com/pod-product-compliance
Lightning Source LLC
Chambersburg PA
CBHW080615110426
42813CB00006B/1515